P9-CKQ-814

the

Allen Hurlburt

gri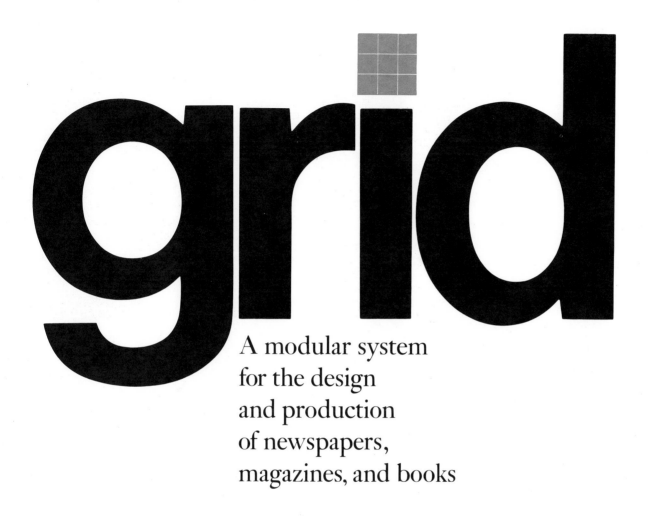d

A modular system
for the design
and production
of newspapers,
magazines, and books

Van Nostrand Reinhold Company
New York

Copyright © 1978 by Allen Hurlburt

Library of Congress Catalog Card Number 78-3734
ISBN 0-442-23966-1

Printed in the United States of America

Van Nostrand Reinhold Company Inc.
115 Fifth Avenue, New York, New York 10003

Van Nostrand Reinhold Australia Pty. Ltd.
480 La Trobe Street
Melbourne, Victoria 3000, Australia

Van Nostrand Reinhold Company Limited
Molly Millars Lane
Wokingham, Berkshire, RG11 2PY England

Macmillan of Canada
Division of Canada Publishing Corporation
164 Commander Boulevard
Agincourt, Ontario M1S 3C7, Canada

16 15 14 13 12 11 10

Library of Congress Cataloging in Publication Data

Hurlburt, Allen, 1910–
    The grid: a modular system for the design and production of newspapers, magazines, and books.

    Bibliography: p.
    Includes index.
    1. Printed, Practical—Layout   I. Title.
Z246.H82   686.2'24   78-3734
ISBN 0-442-23966-1

Foreword

At the outset, it should be pointed out that this book is not an unqualified recommendation of the grid as a primary force in graphic design. Many highly qualified contemporary graphic artists—even in Switzerland and Germany where grid systems originated—are producing outstanding design without the use of formal grids. However, there is ample evidence that modular design in general and grids in particular are influencing the process of design in ways that can no longer be ignored. This book has been written to supply some of that documentation and overcome some of the doubts and confusion that surround this controversial subject.

To demonstrate both the effectiveness and variety of design applications of the grid this book will bring together the work of a selection of outstanding graphic designers whose projects cover a wide spectrum of contemporary design. Through this process it is hoped that the reader will understand the advantages as well as the limitations of the modular approach and then determine the place that the grid should take in his own design. Because the evolutionary growth of modular design systems has never been well documented, some of the ideas and influences that shaped these grids may not be accurately credited to the original source, and I apologize in advance for any such omissions.

Design purists will find much with which to quarrel in some of the grids that appear on the following pages. In this book any combination of horizontal and vertical lines that aids in the solution of a design problem or serves as the foundation of a modular design system qualifies for inclusion as a grid. A distinction will be made between the orthodox grid, in which a network of uniformly spaced horizontal and vertical lines produce a square module, and the more casual typographic grid, in which the primary function of the lines is the identification of margins, column measures, and principal spaces within the design. In a few instances the grids are not much more than the makeup sheets that played an historic role in the development of design systems.

There has never been a time when the graphic designer could disassociate himself or his creative concepts from the reproduction process, and as we move into the new era of computer technology this linkage is even more significant. For that reason the designer will find frequent references in this book to the relationship between design and printing technology. He will also find a "Technical Appendix" and a "Glossary of Computer Terminology" at the end of the book.

It is not difficult to understand why computer-aided design creates anxiety among graphic designers. Today they are challenged by batteries of machines equipped with insatiable appetites for highly structured form and repeatable patterns, when all of their design training and most of their experience has favored innovation and the unexpected. While this problem will continue to plague designers, there are important indications that areas do exist in the design of newspapers, magazines, and books where the designer may be able to make the computer work to his advantage; and in the end he may discover that the computer can absorb some of the chores he never liked in the first place.

Contents

Introduction: 9

With grids by Le Corbusier, Paui Rand, Massimo Vignelli, Josef Müller-Brockmann, and Otl Aicher.

1

Newspapers: 27

With grids by Edwin Taylor, Massimo Vignelli, Frank Ariss, and Alan Fletcher.

2

Magazines: 47

With grids by Massimo Vignelli, Willy Fleckhaus, Will Hopkins, Karl Gerstner, and Walter Bernard.

3

Books: 65

With grids by Jan Tschichold, Bradbury Thompson, Ed Day, and Louis Silverstein.

Technical appendix   81
Glossary of computer terminology   85
Acknowledgments   89
Bibliography   91
Index   93

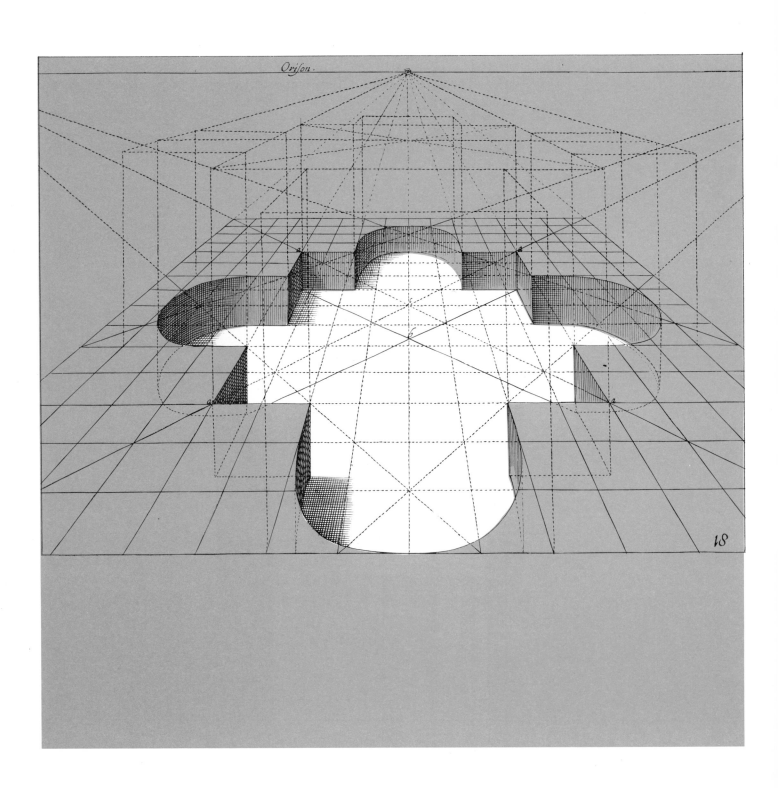

Introduction

The letter G above is from an alphabet by Fra Luca Pacioli with an assist by Leonardo da Vinci for a 1509 book called *De Divina Proportione*. The alphabet is one of the earliest applications of the "golden section" to typographic form. The drawing at the left by Jan de Vries is an example of sixteenth-century use of grid structure to define architectural perspective.

From earliest history man's close kinship with nature has guided him toward a sense of proportion in the shaping of his world. Just as mathematics began with the measurement of objects and space, design began with the arrangement of objects in harmonious relationship to each other and to the space they occupied. The linkage of mathematical systems and design can be traced to the earliest cultures, and science and art have frequently found a common denominator in the search for perfect form throughout history.

Wherever plans have been called for in the building of objects, the division of areas, or the decoration of flat surfaces grids have been involved. Dictionaries define the grid as "a network of uniformly placed horizontal and vertical lines for locating points by means of coordinates." Grids were used by Renaissance artists as a method of scaling their sketches and cartoons to fit the proportions of monolithic murals. Grids are basic to cartography and for centuries military plans have been plotted on the coordinates of grids. Classic architects used grids to plot perspective and scale their plans. From the time of Gutenberg typographers have used grids to design letters and complete the makeup of the printed page.

The factors that distinguish a designer's grid from ordinary makeup sheets are the grid's regard for proportion and its compatibility with the solution to the design problem. There are two ways that the designer can bring mechanical form into harmony with those aesthetic considerations that help to determine the quality of a design. One way is through the use of his own natural and intuitive sense of proportion, and the other is through the application of certain systematic principles of proportion developed by mathematicians, artist-designers, and architects throughout the course of design history.

Most designers prefer to rely on their intuitive sense of proportion in approaching the design problem, but a knowledge of the principles of proportion can be useful in determining the correct division of the space within a layout and assessing the quality of the resulting design. For that reason a brief review of some of the most commonly used rules of proportion will precede and form a background for this exploration of the grid and modular design systems.

By the time civilization had spread across the Aegean Sea and reached its culmination in the acropolis at Athens, clear rules of aesthetic proportion had been laid down. It was Phidias, the master planner of the acropolis, and Ictinus, the architect of the Parthenon, who demonstrated the design potential of the division of a line into an extreme and mean ratio. This was the division of space that was later to be known as the "golden section."

One of the earliest definitive statements of the formal order of aesthetic form was contained in a book written by Fra Luca Pacioli in 1509 called *De Divina Proportione*. The proportion that he called divine is the continual proportion derived from the division of a line into two parts in such a way that the proportion of the full distance to the larger part should correspond geometrically to the proportion of the larger segment to the smaller. When extended, these proportions become a Fibonacci series (named for a thirteenth century mathematician from Pisa). This is a series in which each succeeding number is equal to the sum of the two preceding numbers.

The golden section: This set of proportions is based on the pentagon—a regular five-sided polygon—that together with its related pentagram, or five-pointed star, consists of scores of golden sections. The golden rectangle is constructed with the short side equal to the extreme section of the long side. It is also possible to construct a golden rectangle beginning with the square of the extreme section, as shown in the illustration on page 12.

For those designers who are mathematically inclined, the golden section is an irrational number, 1.61803398, known as Φ—a symbol chosen to represent it in the early twentieth century because it is the first letter in the name of the Greek sculptor and planner, Phidias. The golden section is usually expressed algebraically as $a:b = b:(a+b)$.

The square: The golden section is not the only guide to aesthetic proportion. Several combinations based on the simple square

10

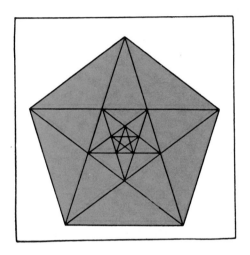

play an important role in the division of space. The square represents a natural division of the golden rectangle, and it provides the base for the root-2 rectangle ($\sqrt{2}$), which is formed by swinging an arc of the diagonal of a square. The resulting rectangle has sometimes been confused with the golden rectangle—a confusion that probably grew out of the activities of a cubist group who used the root-2 rectangle and called their 1912 exhibition in Paris "La Section d'Or." This rectangle provides the basis of the A series of rectangles that is accepted as standard in Europe and the United Kingdom. The common A4 size is 8¼ × 11¾ inches (210 × 297 mm).

The square also plays a key role in the modular

The golden section occurs several times in the theory of regular polygons, polyhedra, and pentagrams (above). The diagram at the right demonstrates one method of dividing a line into an extreme and mean ratio and constructing a golden rectangle. Starting with the line (ab) a triangle is formed using one-half the width of line (ab) as the vertical (bc). The hypotenuse (ac) is then divided by swinging a curve on axis (bc). Using (a) as a centerpoint, swing a curve on axis (as). Where the curve bisects (ab), it will divide the baseline into an extreme (M) and mean (m) proportion. By using (M) as the short side of a rectangle and (ab) as the long side, we have created a golden rectangle.

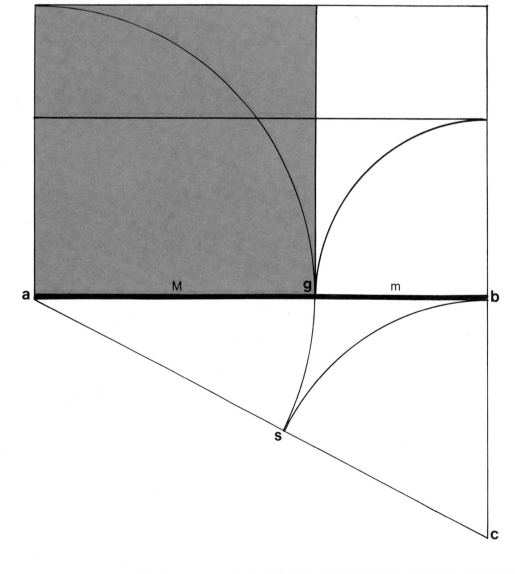

system that grew out of the tatami mat in Japanese domestic architecture. Measuring approximately 3 × 6 feet (.91 × 1.83m), the tatami mat's double-square proportion divided the floor area into a variety of patterns and provided the basis for the splendid asymmetrical form of the traditional Japanese houses.

The square, the simplest of all rectangles, has probably been an even more important factor in the development of the modern designer's grid than the golden

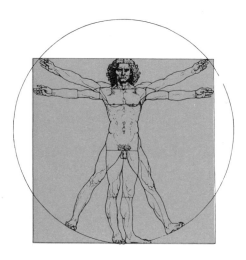

Leonardo's classic drawing establishes the basic symmetry of the square—the principal form of the orthodox grid.

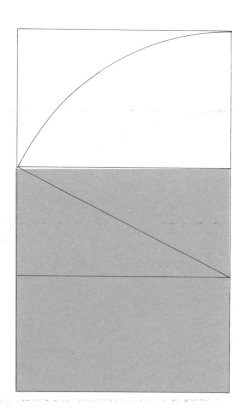

The golden rectangle can be drawn from the square, based on the arc of a diagonal from one corner to a point dividing a side in half.

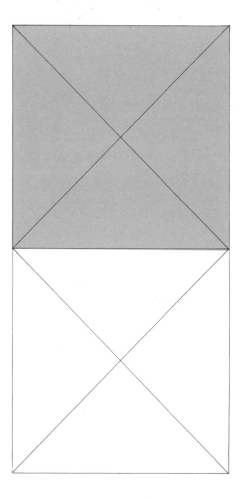

The double square provides the proportion for Japanese tatami mats, which formed the basis for Japanese asymmetrical design.

section or any other system of proportion. Any designer who has had the opportunity to prepare a layout within the square format has found this to be an unusually rewarding experience, even though the shape is uneconomical and impractical for most purposes.

Dynamic symmetry: In the twentieth century two people played a primary role in the revival of the golden section as a design element. One was Jay Hambidge, an author and art instructor, whose book

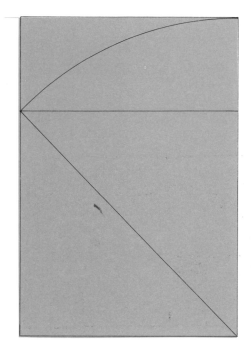

The root-two rectangle is derived from an extension of the square along the arc of its diagonal. This rectangle is sometimes confused with the golden rectangle and it is the basis of the standardized paper sizes in Europe.

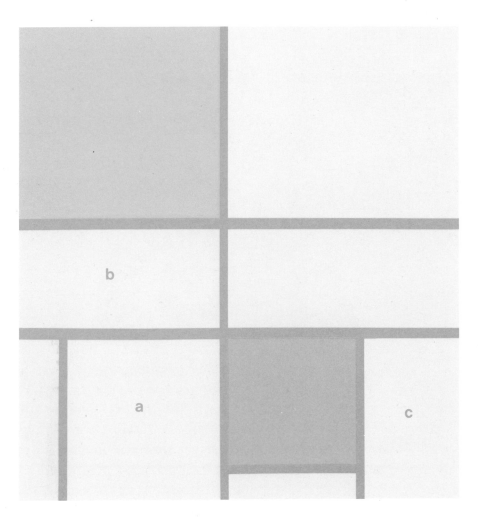

Basic forms are often found in paintings by Piet Mondrian: (a) is a square, (b) is a double square, and (c) is a golden rectangle.

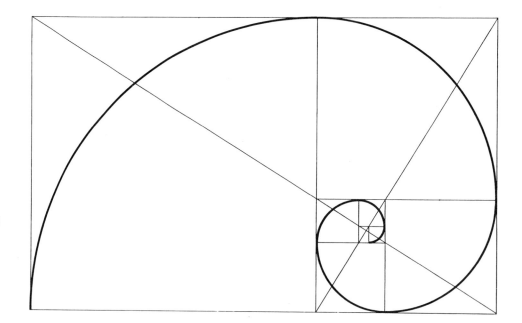

The diagram at the right includes eight golden rectangles in a Fibonacci series positioned to create a logarithmic spiral. The sketches below by Le Corbusier link the spiral to its form in nature and provide the inspiration for his expanding museum plan.

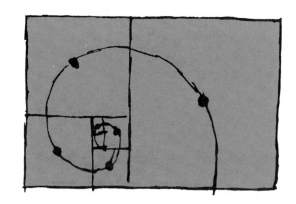

Elements of Dynamic Symmetry was first published in 1920. The other was Le Corbusier, an authentic genius of twentieth century design, who developed the first clearly identifiable design system called the *Modulor*.

    Elements of Dynamic Symmetry is now all but forgotten, but in its time it produced a cultlike mass of followers in the art schools. It was probably Hambidge who first visually linked the golden rectangle to the logarithmic spiral (see above). His writings put a strong emphasis on the diagonal and he developed a series of dynamic rectangles based on a projection of the root-2 rectangle. Hambidge pointed out that the diagonal of a rectangle, when joined with a perpendicular leading to one of the corners created a "harmonic subdivision." He took the expression "dynamic symmetry" from the writings of Plato, and one of his sources of information on classical proportion was the first century B.C. architect and scholar, Vitruvius.

The Modulor: Two thousand years after Vitruvius completed his monumental ten-volume work called *De Architectura*, another architect, Le Corbusier, began to work out a system of architectural proportion called the *Modulor*. Though Le Corbusier does not identify Hambidge as a source of his information on proportion and the logarithmic spiral, he does acknowledge his indebtedness to Matila Ghyka, who in turn was influenced by Hambidge. In any event the *Modulor* made a major contribution to the form of modern architecture and

Le Corbusier developed an elaborate design system based on the golden section and the human proportions. He called his system the *Modulor* and built it around three main points of the anatomy—the top of the head, the solar plexus, and the tip of the raised hand.

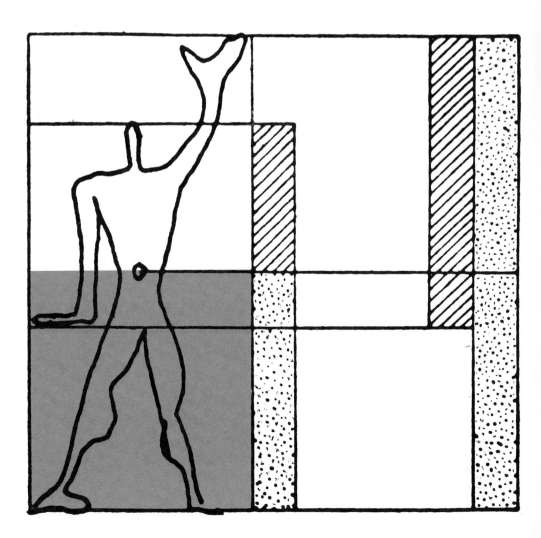

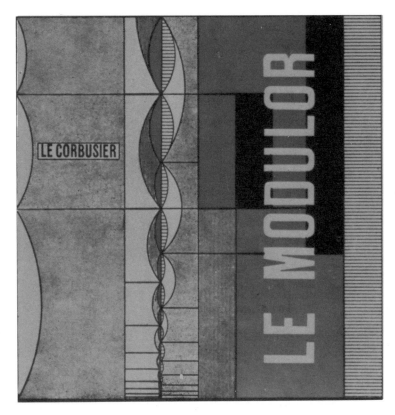

The design for the first book on the *Modulor* was prepared by Le Corbusier using the *Modulor* as a grid. The original was in black, red, and tones and textures of gray.

became the foundation stone for most design systems and modern grids.

Le Corbusier's *Modulor* was primarily concerned with architectural form, but he was quick to point out its application to other areas, including the design of the printed page. This design system took the golden section one step further by linking it to the scale and proportion of the human anatomy. Le Corbusier selected the solar plexus, the top of the head, and the tips of the fingers of an extended arm as the principal anatomical locations. The distance from the ground to the solar plexus represents the extreme division of the golden section, and the distance between the solar plexus and the top of the head is the mean. From this base Le Corbusier produced an infinite series of mathematical proportions that could be applied to a wide range of architectural dimensions.

Most applications of the *Modulor* to graphic design, including Le Corbusier's own designs of *Le Modulor*, *L'Architecture d'Aujourd'hui*, and *Suite de la Modulor*, have not

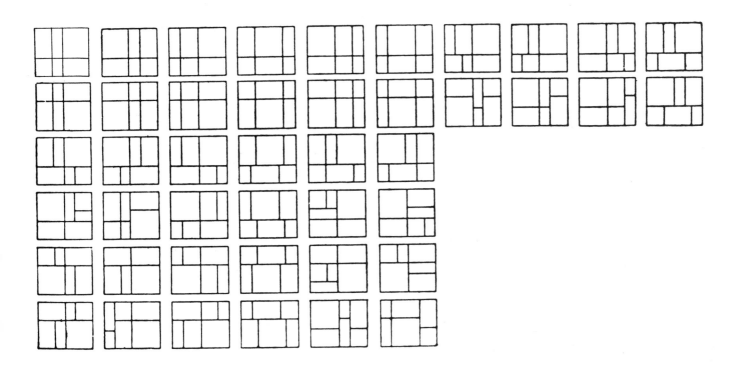

These forty-four divisions of space in a common rectangle were prepared by Le Corbusier to suggest the wide range of options available when designing with the *Modulor*.

been particularly impressive. Perhaps the most important contribution of the *Modulor* to two-dimensional design was the inspiration it gave to the typographic designers of Germany and Switzerland to create the modular systems that would transfer utilitarian makeup sheets to design-oriented modern grids.

The grid: Because the development of the modern grid was an evolutionary process, it is impossible to isolate a single designer as its inventor or accurately list all the pioneers who contributed to the development of modular systems of graphic design. The design schools of the European continent were its principal laboratories, and its influence spread swiftly around the world in the 1950s and 1960s. Over the last three decades the grid has been used by a growing number of graphic designers, frequently with such skill and freedom that a casual observer would never suspect that the design was related to a mechanical form or modular system.

Today the grid has many champions, but it has its

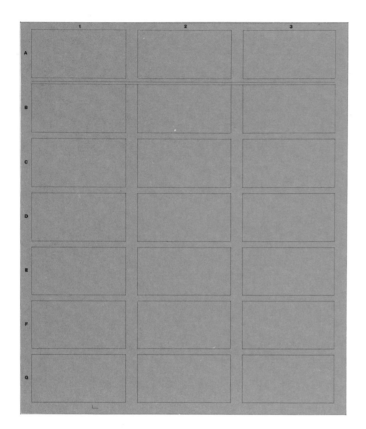

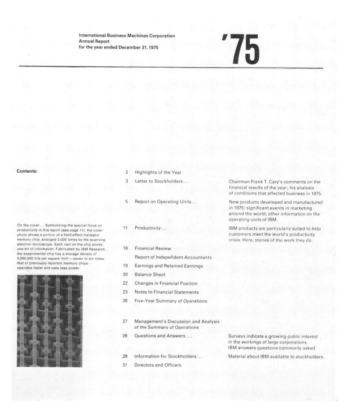

International Business Machines Corporation
Annual Report
for the year ended December 31, 1975

'75

Contents:

2   Highlights of the Year

3   Letter to Stockholders...   Chairman Frank T. Cary's comments on the financial results of the year; his analysis of conditions that affected business in 1975.

5   Report on Operating Units...   New products developed and manufactured in 1975; significant events in marketing around the world; other information on the operating units of IBM.

11   Productivity...   IBM products are particularly suited to help customers meet the world's productivity crisis. Here, stories of the work they do.

18   Financial Review

    Report of Independent Accountants

19   Earnings and Retained Earnings

20   Balance Sheet

22   Changes in Financial Position

23   Notes to Financial Statements

26   Five-Year Summary of Operations

27   Management's Discussion and Analysis of the Summary of Operations

28   Questions and Answers...   Surveys indicate a growing public interest in the workings of large corporations. IBM answers questions commonly asked.

29   Information for Stockholders...   Material about IBM available to stockholders.

31   Directors and Officers

On the cover... Symbolizing the special focus on productivity in this report (see page 11), the cover photo shows a portion of a field-effect transistor memory chip, enlarged 5,000 times by the scanning electron microscope. Each cell on the chip stores one bit of information. Fabricated by IBM Research, the experimental chip has a storage density of 5,000,000 bits per square inch — seven to ten times that of previously reported memory chips — operates faster and uses less power.

Paul Rand's grid for an IBM Annual Report sets a disarmingly simple pattern for the complex range of material that such a publication normally includes in its content.

share of detractors, and it has become a matter of considerable controversy among contemporary designers. When it is used with skill and sensitivity it can lead to the production of handsome and effective pages and it can give the overall design a sense of cohesion and continuity that has a distinctive unifying effect. However, in the hands of a less able designer or when the priority is given to the structure, rather than the creative concept, the grid can become a straitjacket that produces dull layouts and a rigid format.

Learning to prepare and work with the grid is not as complicated as many educators would have us believe, nor is it as simple as some designers pretend. As Paul Rand, America's foremost graphic designer, points out, the explanation of a grid "may seem very simple on the surface, but working with a grid is not so simple. So much depends on the material the designer is called on to incorporate into his designs and the virtually endless surprises he encounters.

Productivity
in IBM

In Sterling Forest, New York, the Field Engineering Division reduces programming workload and improves program quality by using computers at a centralized location.

Productivity improvement, through the use of its own products and the skills of its people, is also an important goal within IBM.

At the Nieder-Roden Distribution Center in Germany, a System/7 controls all imports and exports of the German plants, at significant cost savings. In Endicott, New York, IBM has saved several million dollars by substituting palladium for the gold used in plating pins for printed circuit boards. Endicott also designed and built a new high-speed drilling tool that enables circuit card panels to be drilled in one-fifth the time previously required. In Dayton, New Jersey, a program for reclaiming parts which once were scrapped has saved over $2 million. In Greenock, Scotland, an employee-suggested change in logic design of one IBM product will save the company some $900,000 in 1976.

To optimize production and use of petroleum resources, Indonesia uses computers in refining, distribution and designing expanded capacity.

With the power of word processing at their command, executive and secretary are able to increase efficiency and cut costs.

Right: East Fishkill, New York, a mobile elevator system for warehouse storage and retrieval saved over $300,000 the first year.

Solving a design problem is much like running a maze. The designer selects a line to follow only to learn that the constraints he encounters send him back to probe another direction until he finds a clear path to the solution. The application of the grid to his design procedure presents similar problems. If the designer formulates a grid before he has arrived at a design concept, he may well find that he has blocked the way to the correct solution. In the following paragraphs I will list some of the priorities in designing with grids, but in the final analysis each designer will have to work out his own procedure to suit his thought process, working methods, and personal style.

1. At the foundation of any modular approach to design is a firm understanding of the communication problem, from its objectives to the potential response of its readers. He will need to know what constraints are inherent to the project,

19

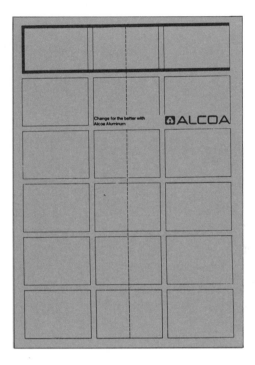

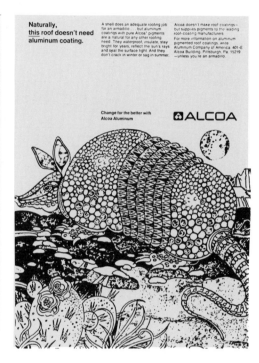

such as space, time, and the inevitable budget.

2. Before serious designing can begin, the designer should have an accurate measurement of the physical requirements: the nature of the visual material and the space it will occupy, the order and continuity best suited to the presentation of the content, and the degree of emphasis that each element may require. This calls for value judgements. It is not just the number of words and images, but the degree of emphasis given to them, that will eventually determine the value of visual communication.

3. The next step in the design process is the distillation of all the forces into a single design concept. It is at this point that the grid will most frequently enter the designer's thinking, though it may enter at earlier or even later stages. In any event, it should be clear that the grid and modular systems should serve the idea and not lead it. When grid structures dominate the creative process there is a real danger that a rigid solution may result.

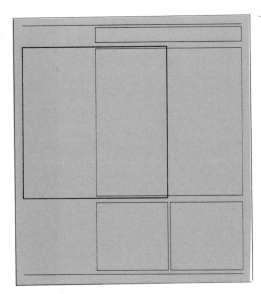

The grid above was designed by Josef Müller-Brockmann for a series of advertisements like the one at the right. The grid on the facing left page was one of several designed by Massimo Vignelli for Alcoa Aluminum advertisements.

4. As the designer turns to the form of the grid he will seek the same simplicity in its structure that he sought in the design concept. The grid may take many forms. It may merely define the margins and type columns or it may provide a complex framework for a wide range of typographic options and visual opportunities. In any event, it will be judged by the quality of the resulting design and not by the intricate tracery of its own form.

Form and function: The pattern of a grid will be guided by the function of the content and the design concept. Because each grid is custom-made to fit the parameters of a specific project and because its design is governed by the particular working style of an individual designer, grids will take on an almost unlimited variation in form. However, there are a few general principles that apply to most grids and these will be useful to the designer in preparing modular systems.

The *orthodox design grid*, which forms the basis of the

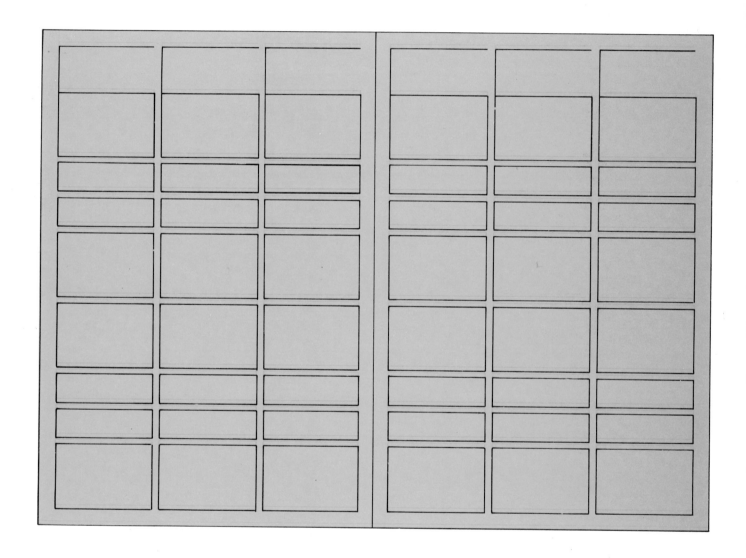

modular design systems that were developed in Ulm, Basle, and Zurich during the years after the war, is based on a uniformly spaced combination of horizontal and vertical lines that produce a pattern of squares similar to those on a graph sheet. This grid calls for the not-always-easy-to-attain standardization of the horizontal and vertical measurements based on the line-space (type height plus the space between the lines) of the dominant text face. For example, if the type is 10 point with 2 points between lines, the basic measurement is 12 points, or 1 pica. If the type column is 14 picas

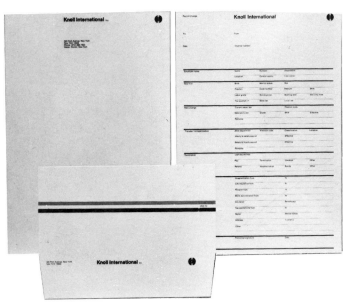

Sometimes a single grid can serve several different purposes. The grid on the facing page was designed by Massimo Vignelli for Knoll International to control a total identification program that consisted of forms, letterheads, catalogues, price lists, and brochures, a few examples of which are shown above and right.

wide with 1 pica between columns, the grid will divide into 14 pica squares with 1 pica of separation. If a 48-point type is used for the headlines, each line will take four increments of space, and if a 6-point type is used for captions, each line of caption type will take half a line.

In practice it is not always possible to divide the grid into squares, but designers working with grids should understand the advantages of this approach. A pattern of squares on a page is not only an ideal base for a modular structure, but it also groups naturally into horizontal and vertical rectangles in the proportions of 1 × 2, 2 × 3, and 3 × 4.

The vertical lines of a grid will control the inner and outer margins, define the type columns, and determine the space separating them. The positioning of these lines will be nearly always measured in picas and half picas to correspond with existing typographic standards.

The horizontal lines of the grid will determine the head and foot margins, the depth of the type columns, and

The remarkable signage system on the facing page was designed by Otl Aicher, an early exponent of grids in Germany, for the Munich Olympic games. It was based on a grid (left) and interchangeable elements forming a body alphabet.

the location of the headlines and visual material. Unlike the vertical lines that are normally positioned according to pica measurements, the horizontal lines are often spaced on the basis of line-spaces (a 9-point type with 1-point leading will yield a 10-point increment). This is one of the reasons a perfectly square grid is not always possible.

In some publications the grid may be expected to provide for several different column widths. It is possible to add as many vertical lines as are necessary even though they produce a random pattern, but many designers prefer to work within a more tightly structured modular system where the different column widths are all provided for. Several grids in this book show how this multiunit system works.

Note: In this book the term "unit" used to define grids will apply to column widths. A six-unit grid will identify a grid that provides for a maximum of six columns, etc. Other writers have used several other methods of identifying grids.

The grid assumes its most important design function when the vertical and horizontal lines combine to produce

the squares or rectangles that form a blueprint for the printed page. In the design process the working grids can take several different forms. The grid may be an actual size overlay rendered on tracing paper or transparent acetate, or it can be an underlay that shows through the layout sheets.

Many designers like to make their preliminary sketches on sizes smaller than the finished page. On magazines it is common practice to work on one-quarter or one-third scale grids. Similar or even smaller sizes are often used for the thumbnail layouts of book pages. In the planning of newspaper pages the working grids are usually half scale.

Most final layouts and mechanical paste-ups are prepared on actual-size grid sheets. These are usually printed in blue ink. In the future some working grids may be adapted to computerized systems, where they will guide the final layout on visual display terminals, or they may even be fed into terminals to prepare pages in a fully automated preset program.

In recent years the grid has been used to solve a wide range of design problems. It has been an important aid in the preparation of annual reports, brochures, directories, catalogues, sign systems, advertising campaigns, and corporate identification programs. The grids accompanying this introduction illustrate a few applications of the grid to areas other than publication design.

It may be appropriate to close this introduction to the grid with a few words of caution. Josef Müller-Brockmann, a Swiss designer noted for the clarity and graphic form of his designs, maintains that the "grid system is an aid, not a guarantee. It permits a number of possible uses and each designer can look for a solution appropriate to his personal style. But one must learn how to use the grid; it is an art that requires practice." As a final note of caution, Le Corbusier in his comments about the design system he called the *Modulor* points out, "I still reserve the right, at any time, to doubt the solutions furnished by the *Modular*, keeping intact my freedom, which must depend on my feelings rather than my reason."

1. newspapers

The logotype of the *Times* of London was changed from Gothic (Old English) style lettering to Times Roman when the format and typeface were restyled by Stanley Morison in 1931.

The design of the format of the *Times* has been gradually evolving in the years since 1931. It wasn't until thirty years later that the front page abandoned its traditional mass of classified advertisements on page one. Since then its design editor, Jeanette Collins, has welded the format into its modular form.

Reading habits have made the central fold of modern broadsheet newspapers a critical factor in the division of space. Designers usually avoid breaking headlines or key parts of photographs above and below this important dividing line.

In recent years brief summaries of news items appearing on the inside pages of a newspaper have become a major feature of the front page.

Newspapers

Without even knowing it, most newspapers use a grid system in their makeup. The very nature of column divisions, rules, and prescribed headline counts becomes its own modular system. But without design considerations these systems become self-limiting. Unfortunately, design considerations have generally held a low priority in newspaper publishing and, with a few notable exceptions, the result has been a cluttered jungle of newsprint.

For many years the clean typography and organized pages of the *New York Herald Tribune* provided almost the only relief from this clutter. Much of this clarity and freshness is retained in the International edition, which is still published in Paris. The *Herald Tribune* made still another contribution to newspaper design in the 1960s when its Sunday edition was restyled by Peter Palazzo, a skilled graphic designer with a background in advertising and promotional design. He was one of the first designers to point out that the grid (makeup sheet) traditionally used by newspapers "for reasons of efficiency" also acts as a modular organizing element for the design of effective newspaper pages. Peter Palazzo's designs with their dramatic use of photography, illustration, and typography set a new tone for the design of newspapers. Although the program came too late to rescue the *Herald Tribune* from already severe financial difficulties, Peter Palazzo's layouts went on to influence the design of newspapers, supplements, and magazines.

Another important development in newspaper design took place nearly three decades earlier in 1932 when Stanley Morison restyled the *Times* of London and created a revolution in typography with the introduction of Times Roman. This program had a greater influence on typography than on the overall design of newspaper formats, but one significant change was the replacement of the tired Gothic (Old English) logotype with the clean Times Roman letters based on classic forms. Stanley Morison's typeface went on to become one of the most popular text faces designed in this century. Ironically, Times Roman, which was designed for newspapers, has had its greatest success as a book and magazine typeface.

There have been many other important changes in newspaper design, and this section will cover some of the most significant ones, but it is impossible to include all of the incidents that have had a bearing on the look of the modern newspaper. As a background for a study of the grid and its relationship to newspapers, it may be useful to examine some of the major shifts that have taken place in newspaper publishing in recent years.

For many years newspaper pages were made up of tightly stacked columns of text with the headlines compressed between typographic rules. This created highly structured, but dull, pages. In the 1930s newspapers began to move away from this pattern and gradually a more horizontal influence began to take over. This move was partly inspired by the new type of content and by a desire for stronger and less condensed headlines.

With the trend away from vertical emphasis, many newspapers eliminated column rules. For a time this was considered to be the last word in "modern" newspaper design, but in many cases this was a mixed blessing. Harold Evans, editor of the *London Sunday Times*, takes a dim view of this trend in his excellent book *Editing and Design—Book 5*. He writes, "The most backward step, under the flag of freedom, has been the abandonment of column rules and cutoffs which so usefully define columns and separate stories." Harold Evans' objections notwithstanding, most newspapers have elected to separate their columns with 1 pica of space rather than the traditional hairline rule.

In recent years newspapers have been taking a fresh look at the traditional narrow columns that make up their pages. Most American newspapers used an eight-column makeup for their news pages until the 1960s when a trend set in toward wider column measures. Since then, an increasing number of dailies have shifted to six-column makeup. Along with the reexamination of column widths came a reappraisal of type sizes. Nine-point has been gradually replacing the traditional 7- and 8-point sizes. Behind these shifts in type size there is a concern for legibility. The optimum text line for ease of reading is 15 picas, and the optimum typeface for

Peter Palazzo's impressive redesign of the Sunday edition of the *New York Herald Tribune* in the early 1960s represented one of the first applications of traditional makeup sheets to modular page design.

this measure is 9 point with a character count of about forty-five letters. The 9-point type also brings the typography in line with magazines. There have been a few experiments with unjustified settings with a ragged right-hand margin, but so far none of these have been notably successful.

Perhaps one of the most dramatic changes in newspaper design has been the new approach to headline typography. In traditional newspaper makeup, display type was trapped in the narrow column framework, where it became more and more condensed. The general style was called "decker," and it consisted of several layers, or decks, of diminishing type sizes that gradually led down to the dateline and the beginning of the article. These headlines were often set in capitals. In the 1930s newspapers began to experiment with upper- and lowercase headlines that were aligned at the left and spread over two or more columns. Today this has become the basic style for headlines, although too many newspapers persist in following the archaic style of capitalizing the first letter of nearly all words when simple, normal word capitalization would be easier to read and the letters

The special feature pages of the daily *London Times* have served as experimental proving grounds for typographic innovation and fresh approaches to overall form.

would take less space.

In a study of this dimension it is impossible to single out everyone who has influenced newspaper design or contributed to the modular approach to page makeup. It is important, though, to examine the work of a few key designers in order to understand the growing importance of the grid and its role in future design development.

The contribution of Peter Palazzo's redesign of the *Sunday Herald Tribune* and his identification of traditional makeup sheets as modular organizers of newspaper content has already been cited (see page 29). Since the 1960s, several other designers have worked with grids to revitalize the design of newspapers. These redesign programs have been achieved in two different ways—from the inside and from the outside. The external approach depends on the use of design consultants, the advantages being a fresh viewpoint and proven talent on the part of the consultant, but the disadvantage being a limited knowledge of the newspaper's special problems. Such programs are sometimes devised to please advertisers, rather than readers, and this creates a conflict between the editors and the designer. The internal redesign program has the advantage of a close working relationship between the design staff and the editors, but it depends on the quality of the designers and their freedom from the inhibiting factor of internal pressures. One of the important advantages of an inside program is the opportunity for a gradual and transitional reshaping of the content.

Two of the world's leading newspapers, the *Times* of London and the *New York Times*, have made effective use of internal design staffs. It wasn't until 1966 that the *London Times* abandoned its traditional custom of filling the front page with classified notices. But from that point on it moved gradually toward a handsome, well-organized format under the direction of design editor, Jeanette Collins. The typography is still wedded to Morison's Times Roman and the headlines are uniform in weight and aligned at the left with occasional contrasting symmetrical type arrangements. Bold rules are used to add horizontal emphasis to the pages.

From the beginning, the *London Sunday Times* has been

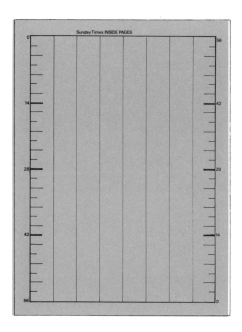

The *London Sunday Times*, under the design direction of Edwin Taylor, has used modular design to achieve a bold and varied typographic approach, although its makeup sheets lack the guidance and control of a designer's grid.

a completely separate newspaper from the daily, and, until recently, it was owned by a different publisher. It was not a party to Morison's redesign, but in recent years it has been restyled into an exciting and impressive format by Harold Evans, its editor, and Edwin Taylor, its design director.

The *New York Times* has clung to the past with a bit more tenacity than its London counterpart. Until recently, its front page was one of the last bastions of decker headlines. In the late 1960s the *Times*' director of design, Louis Silverstein, directed his attention to the design of the pages of the daily and Sunday editions. His six-column, asymmetrical layouts for the op ed pages with strong graphic illustrations set the wheels of change in motion at the *Times* and went on to influence the treatment of this kind of content at other newspapers. Lou Silverstein worked gradually through the special sections and feature pages of the Sunday edition and the interior feature pages of the daily *Times*. He left revision of the news pages until last, and in 1976 the *Times* made a major change from eight columns to six.

Elmhurst to
Manhattan—
One Classic Style

The New York Times

THE

Home

SECTION

Instant Furniture
Boom: The Latest
Look Is Sophisticated,
The Assembly Is Easy
Page C4

The sun helps bring
heating costs down
to earth in Connecticut — **8**

Television:
Lynn Redgrave
on her new career — **29**

Books: A look at
human behavior
and Virginia Woolf — **32**

White House Acquisitor

How to cope when your apartment's unfinished. Joan Kron on interim decorating. Page C16.

Under the creative guidance of Louis Silverstein, the *New York Times* has been producing some exciting newspaper pages. Special sections of the Sunday edition (above) and daily sections like "Home" (right) serve as testing areas for the gradual reshaping of this monolithic newspaper.

34

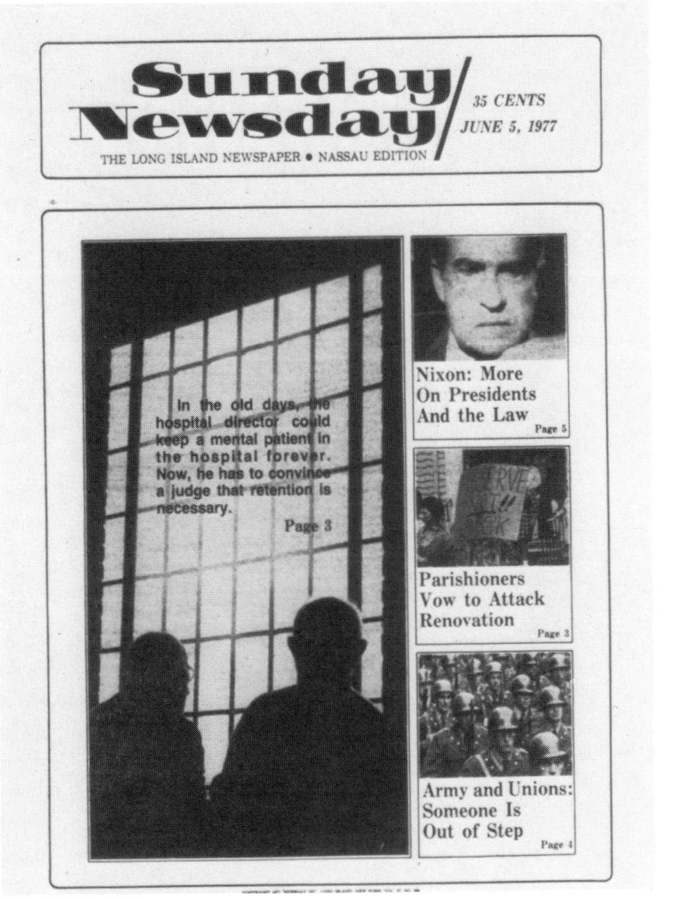

Sunday Newsday

35 CENTS

JUNE 5, 1977

THE LONG ISLAND NEWSPAPER • NASSAU EDITION

In the old days, the hospital director could keep a mental patient in the hospital forever. Now, he has to convince a judge that retention is necessary.

Page 3

Nixon: More On Presidents And the Law

Page 5

Parishioners Vow to Attack Renovation

Page 3

Army and Unions: Someone Is Out of Step

Page 4

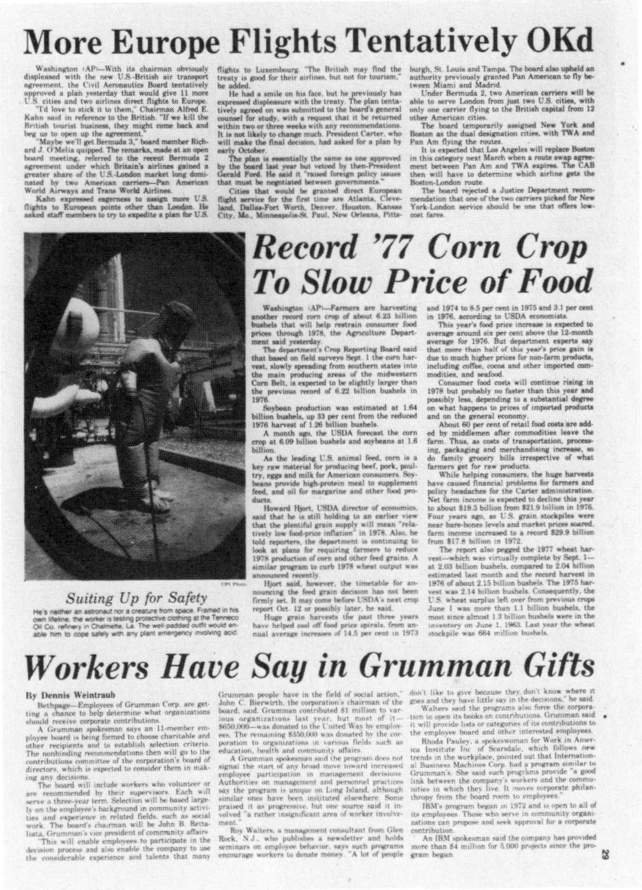

More Europe Flights Tentatively OKd

Washington (AP)—With its chairman obviously displeased with the new U.S.-British air transport agreement, the Civil Aeronautics Board tentatively approved a plan yesterday that would give 11 more U.S. cities and two airlines direct flights to Europe.

"I'd love to stick it to them," Chairman Alfred E. Kahn said in reference to the British. "If we kill the British tourist business, they might come back and beg us to open up the agreement."

"Maybe we'll get Bermuda 3," board member Richard J. O'Melia quipped. The remarks, made at an open board meeting, referred to the recent Bermuda 2 agreement under which Britain's airlines gained a greater share of the U.S.-London market long dominated by two American carriers—Pan American World Airways and Trans World Airlines.

Kahn expressed eagerness to assign more U.S. flights to European points other than London. He asked staff members to try to expedite a plan for U.S. flights to Luxembourg. "The British may find the treaty is good for their airlines, but not for tourism," he added.

He had a smile on his face, but he previously has expressed displeasure with the treaty. The plan tentatively agreed on was submitted to the board's general counsel for study, with a request that it be returned within two or three weeks with any recommendations. It is not likely to change much. President Carter, who will make the final decision, had asked for a plan by early October.

The plan is essentially the same as one approved by the board last year but vetoed by then-President Gerald Ford. He said it "raised foreign policy issues that must be negotiated between governments."

Cities that would be granted direct European flight service for the first time are Atlanta, Cleveland, Dallas-Fort Worth, Denver, Houston, Kansas City, Mo., Minneapolis-St. Paul, New Orleans, Pittsburgh, St. Louis and Tampa. The board also upheld an authority previously granted Pan American to fly between Miami and Madrid.

Under Bermuda 2, two American carriers will be able to serve London from just two U.S. cities, with only one carrier flying to the British capital from 12 other American cities.

The board temporarily assigned New York and Boston as the dual designation cities, with TWA and Pan Am flying the routes.

It is expected that Los Angeles will replace Boston in this category next March when a route swap agreement between Pan Am and TWA expires. The CAB then will have to determine which airline gets the Boston-London route.

The board rejected a Justice Department recommendation that one of the two carriers picked for New York-London service should be one that offers low-cost fares.

UPI Photo

Suiting Up for Safety

He's neither an astronaut nor a creature from space. Framed in his own lifeline, the worker is testing protective clothing at the Tenneco Oil Co. refinery in Chalmette, La. The well-padded outfit would enable him to cope safely with any plant emergency involving acid.

Record '77 Corn Crop To Slow Price of Food

Washington (AP)—Farmers are harvesting another record corn crop of about 6.23 billion bushels that will help restrain consumer food prices through 1978, the Agriculture Department said yesterday.

The department's Crop Reporting Board said that based on field surveys Sept. 1 the corn harvest, slowly spreading from southern states into the main producing areas of the midwestern Corn Belt, is expected to be slightly larger than the previous record of 6.22 billion bushels in 1976.

Soybean production was estimated at 1.64 billion bushels, up 33 per cent from the reduced 1976 harvest of 1.26 billion bushels.

A month ago, the USDA forecast the corn crop at 6.09 billion bushels and soybeans at 1.6 billion.

As the leading U.S. animal feed, corn is a key raw material for producing beef, pork, poultry, eggs and milk for American consumers. Soybeans provide high-protein meal to supplement feed, and oil for margarine and other food products.

Howard Hjort, USDA director of economics, said that he is still holding to an earlier view that the plentiful grain supply will mean "relatively low food-price inflation" in 1978. Also, he told reporters, the department is continuing to look at plans for requiring farmers to reduce 1978 production of corn and other feed grains. A similar program to curb 1978 wheat output was announced recently.

Hjort said, however, the timetable for announcing the feed grain decision has not been firmly set. It may come before USDA's next crop report Oct. 12 or possibly later, he said.

Huge grain harvests the past three years have helped cool off food price spirals, from annual average increases of 14.5 per cent in 1973 and 1974 to 8.5 per cent in 1975 and 3.1 per cent in 1976, according to USDA economists.

This year's food price increase is expected to average around six per cent above the 12-month average for 1976. But department experts say that more than half of this year's price gain is due to much higher prices for non-farm products, including coffee, cocoa and other imported commodities, and seafood.

Consumer food costs will continue rising in 1978 but probably no faster than this year and possibly less, depending to a substantial degree on what happens to prices of imported products and on the general economy.

About 60 per cent of retail food costs are added by middlemen after commodities leave the farm. Thus, as costs of transportation, processing, packaging and merchandising increase, so do family grocery bills irrespective of what farmers get for raw products.

While helping consumers, the huge harvests have caused financial problems for farmers and policy headaches for the Carter administration. Net farm income is expected to decline this year to about $19.3 billion from $21.9 billion in 1976. Four years ago, as U.S. grain stockpiles were near bare-bones levels and market prices soared, farm income increased to a record $29.9 billion from $17.8 billion in 1972.

The report also pegged the 1977 wheat harvest—which was virtually complete by Sept. 1—at 2.03 billion bushels, compared to 2.04 billion estimated last month and the record harvest in 1976 of about 2.15 billion bushels. The 1975 harvest was 2.14 billion bushels. Consequently, the U.S. wheat surplus left over from previous crops June 1 was more than 1.1 billion bushels, the most since almost 1.3 billion bushels were in the inventory on June 1, 1963. Last year the wheat stockpile was 664 million bushels.

Workers Have Say in Grumman Gifts

By Dennis Weintraub

Bethpage—Employees of Grumman Corp. are getting a chance to help determine what organizations should receive corporate contributions.

A Grumman spokesman says an 11-member employee board is being formed to choose charitable and other recipients and to establish selection criteria. The nonbinding recommendations then will go to the contributions committee of the corporation's board of directors, which is expected to consider them in making any decisions.

The board will include workers who volunteer or are recommended by their supervisors. Each will serve a three-year term. Selection will be based largely on the employee's background in community activities and experience in related fields, such as social work. The board's chairman will be John B. Rettaliata, Grumman's vice president of community affairs.

"This will enable employees to participate in the decision process and also enable the company to use the considerable experience and talents that many Grumman people have in the field of social action," John C. Bierwirth, the corporation's chairman of the board, said. Grumman contributed $1 million to various organizations last year, but most of it—$650,000—was donated to the United Way by employees. The remaining $350,000 was donated by the corporation to organizations in various fields such as education, health and community affairs.

A Grumman spokesman said the program does not signal the start of any broad move toward increased employee participation in management decisions. Authorities on management and personnel practices say the program is unique on Long Island, although similar ones have been instituted elsewhere. Some praised it as progressive, but one source said it involved "a rather insignificant area of worker involvement."

Roy Walters, a management consultant from Glen Rock, N.J., who publishes a newsletter and holds seminars on employee behavior, says such programs encourage workers to donate money. "A lot of people don't like to give because they don't know where it goes and they have little say in the decisions," he said.

Walters said the programs also force the corporation to open its books on contributions. Grumman said it will provide lists or categories of its contributions to the employee board and other interested employees.

Rhoda Pauley, a spokeswoman for Work in America Institute Inc. of Scarsdale, which follows new trends in the workplace, pointed out that International Business Machines Corp. had a program similar to Grumman's. She said such programs provide "a good link between the company's workers and the communities in which they live. It moves corporate philanthropy from the board room to employees."

IBM's program began in 1972 and is open to all of its employees. Those who serve in community organizations can propose and seek approval for a corporate contribution.

An IBM spokesman said the company has provided more than $4 million for 5,000 projects since the program began.

29

Paul Back's design for *Newsday*, a surburban newspaper in Long Island, New York, set a new style for the half-size (tabloid) newspaper. These layouts, based on a three- and four-column grid, apply news magazine design to the newspaper.

So far, the newspapers under consideration have been full-size (broadsheet) format. For about one hundred years there have also been half-size (tabloid) newspapers, and, for the most part, they have been more concerned with the blackness of their headlines and the boldness of their statements than with the quality of their design. There have been exceptions, and one the most notable of these is *Newsday*, a highly successful suburban newspaper published in Nassau County, Long Island. Redesigned in 1968 by its director of design, Paul Back, the layout takes on the serious, almost restrained, tone of a news magazine and stands out against the blatant confusion of most tabloids. The module is based on a three- and four-column makeup and it uses

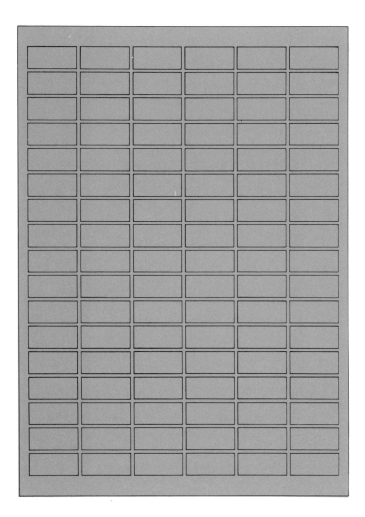

An outstanding example of modern newspaper design was the *Herald*, a New York Sunday newspaper that was introduced in 1971. This handsome format was created by Massimo Vignelli, using the six-unit grid (above) divided into 102 double-square rectangles.

occasional ruled boxes with round corners. One of the unique features of the format is the way it organizes the advertising content. Small advertisements are grouped into single-page or rectangular units that do not intrude on the editorial space.

All of the redesign programs covered so far have been the work of internal staffs. Those that follow will demonstrate the work of independent design consultants, who have been brought in to analyze the design problem and work with the publisher and editorial staff to arrive at a solution.

In 1971 Massimo Vignelli, a graphic designer with an international reputation, was called on to design a new Sunday newspaper for New York City called the *Herald*. He created a modular grid for the format with many unique

The large-page size of the *Herald* had a strong horizontal emphasis with bold (6-point) rules marking the major divisions, and 2-point rules separating articles. Massimo Vignelli's format returned to the functional hairline column rules that most newspapers have abandoned.

These pages from the *Herald* under-
score the variety of design solutions
possible with the grid structure.
The design system also took into
account optimum line lengths for
ease of reading, and it was planned
to accommodate computer-directed
production techniques.

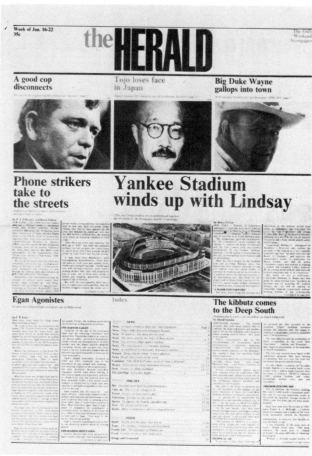

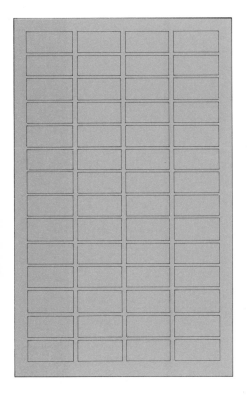

The *Sunday Herald* was divided into four parts. There were two full-size sections to cover the news and two half-size sections called "Issue" and "Inside" to function as magazines. These tabloid sections were laid out on a grid consisting of four columns and fourteen horizontal divisions.

features. The creative key to the grid was its carefully planned horizontal division of space. This brought complete modular control to the design of the pages without limiting the ability of the format to accommodate all manner of material, including the endless miscellanea that every issue of a newspaper must have.

The large page size, 17 × 22½ inches (431 × 570mm), had a grid that provided for six columns with six vertical divisions and seventeen horizontal divisions. One of the unusual features of Massimo Vignelli's grid was the return to light rules to divide the columns. This format was also designed to take advantage of computerized composition and automated page makeup when the process became available. Although the *Herald* was to have a short life as a newspaper, its design was a near perfect application of the grid to newspaper design and its format will continue to influence

The format for the *Minneapolis Tribune* designed by Frank Ariss is based on a modular system that he refers to as "design engineering." The display typeface is Helvetica. The grid originally in eight units was later revised to six (page 42).

the redesign of modern newspapers.

The same year that Massimo Vignelli designed the format for the *Herald* in New York, Frank Ariss, who had studied designing with grids at London's Royal College of Art, undertook an extensive redesign program for the *Minneapolis Tribune*. This design project was backed by two years of planning, and it is based on a grid with precise vertical and horizontal measurements providing accurate spaces for the Helvetica headlines and the columns of 9-point type with ½-point space between the lines.

Frank Ariss calls his approach "graphic engineering" and his program was planned to dovetail into the extensive computerization that the *Minneapolis Tribune* was then undergoing. The redesign has resulted in a remarkably clean, if somewhat dogmatic, presentation and has led to significant time savings and economies in type composition, makeup, and press handling.

One interesting change in this new format was the

The text typography of the *Minneapolis Tribune* follows the Swiss precedent by substituting one line of space for the more traditional paragraph indentation. Special sections like "Thursday" are sometimes set in an unjustified style.

Units 9 1|2	Page		Inches	
2				
4				
6				
8	1	21	21	
10				
12				
14	2	20	20	
16				
18				
20				
22	3	19	19	
24				
26				
28				
30	4	18	18	
32				
34				
36				
38	5	17	17	
40				
42				
44				
46	6	16	16	
48				
50				
52				
54	7	15	15	
56				
58				
60				
62	8	14	14	
64				
66				
68	9	13	13	
70				
72				
74				
76	10	12	12	
78				
80				
82				
84	11	11	11	
86				
88				
90				
92	12	10	10	
94				
96				
98	13	9	9	
100				
102				
104				
106	14	8	8	
108				
110				
112				
114	15	7	7	
116				
118				
120				
122	16	6	6	
124				
126				
128	17	5	5	
130				
132				
134				
136	18	4	4	
138				
140				
142				
144	19	3	3	
146				
148				
150				
152	20	2	2	
154				
156				
158				
160	21	1	1	
162				
164				
166				
	22			

The grid at the left is the one Frank Ariss designed for the *Minneapolis Tribune*, reproduced in the commonly used reduction of half scale (1 en equals 1 em). There are two scales for the vertical measurement. The one on the left is based on line units of 9-point type with ½-point line space. The other is in inches to accommodate the entrenched habit of editors and journalists to measure the length of articles in inches.

This is a prototype page (right) from a design proposal Frank Ariss prepared for the *San Francisco Examiner* in 1973, using a grid that was identical to the one on the left.

Examiner

San Francisco

1st edition
Evening/15cents/No 32/109th year

Wednesday 18
July 1973

Led Zeppelin/
Their enormous popularity and bankroll/35

Wild Watergate payoff tales

Tony Ulasewicz spills the beans

Showdown/Can Cox get evidence he wants from the White House?

Special prosecutor Cox relaxes with his newspaper during early morning walk

Kalmbach thinks he acted illegally

Pulse

Phase IV today—may jack up food prices

The President gets back to work

Violence renewed in Northern Ireland

The season of our indignation

BART talks stymied. strike continues

How our kids get along in school

An interview with an IRA priest, who says the conflict is not a religious war/32

Pacific Heights wins a high-rise battle

Did voiceprints nab the wrong man?

Tax rollback?/7
On the trail with LA's new mayor/20
SF's biggest heroin bust ever/24
How to scream/32
The dollar sags/39
Vida Blue wins, then whines/55
Cyclists lament/57

1st section
Bay/4
California 7
National/8
International/17
Dimension/20
Editorial/22
Weather/24
Crime/24

Scene
Entertainments/34
What's going on 38

Money
Stocks/41
Want ads/43
Obituaries/54

Sports
Racing/61
Comics/62
TV Radio/63

Weather
coastal fog

Bay smog index
North
Central
South

Alan Fletcher's design for *24 Ore*, an Italian newspaper similar to the *Wall Street Journal* and the *Financial Times*, is based on a unique nine-unit grid supported by a strong horizontal emphasis.

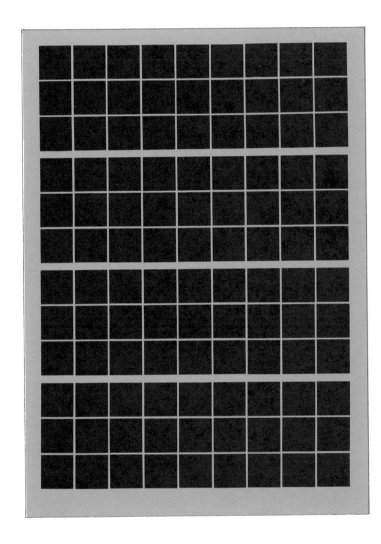

The grid (above) and the type specimen sheet at the right are reproduced from the forty-eight-page design manual of *24 Ore*. These pages demonstrate how the nine-unit modular system can be used to create three different column widths with six variations in the form of major and minor features.

adoption of the English tradition of placing the most important page-one story at the left, rather than the right—the standard location in most American newspapers. The format contains several other typographic innovations: instead of paragraph indentations, a line of space separates paragraphs; articles that fall a few lines short on the runover are allowed to remain that way; and headlines use capital letters only where sentence structure calls for uppercase.

A year after the introduction of the *Minneapolis Tribune* format, Frank Ariss undertook a redesign program for the *San Francisco Examiner*. Based on the same grid format, this proposed redesign extended his ideas of newspaper typography one step further by using a sans-serif typeface for the text as well as the headlines. A prototype of the *Examiner* was produced in July of 1973.

Another interesting example of newspaper redesign is Alan Fletcher's new format for *24 Ore* (24 Hours), an Italian financial daily. The nine-unit grid that he selected for his modular is unusual, but it accommodates an extensive number of different column widths that give variety to the format and permit the editors to handle the varied content common to this type of journal. In the design systems manual the varying column measures are keyed to text sizes, headline styles, and photographic cropping, all of which are tied to a modular structure, relating all of the design elements to each other and to the overall format. In discussing the new format for *24 Ore*, Alan Fletcher, a design partner of London's Pentagram Studio, notes that "the design of a daily newspaper is a difficult undertaking. Compromise on the niceties of typography is inevitable, control of layout minimal, and perfection unobtainable. The graphic style has to be forceful and distinctive to be visible."

2. magazines

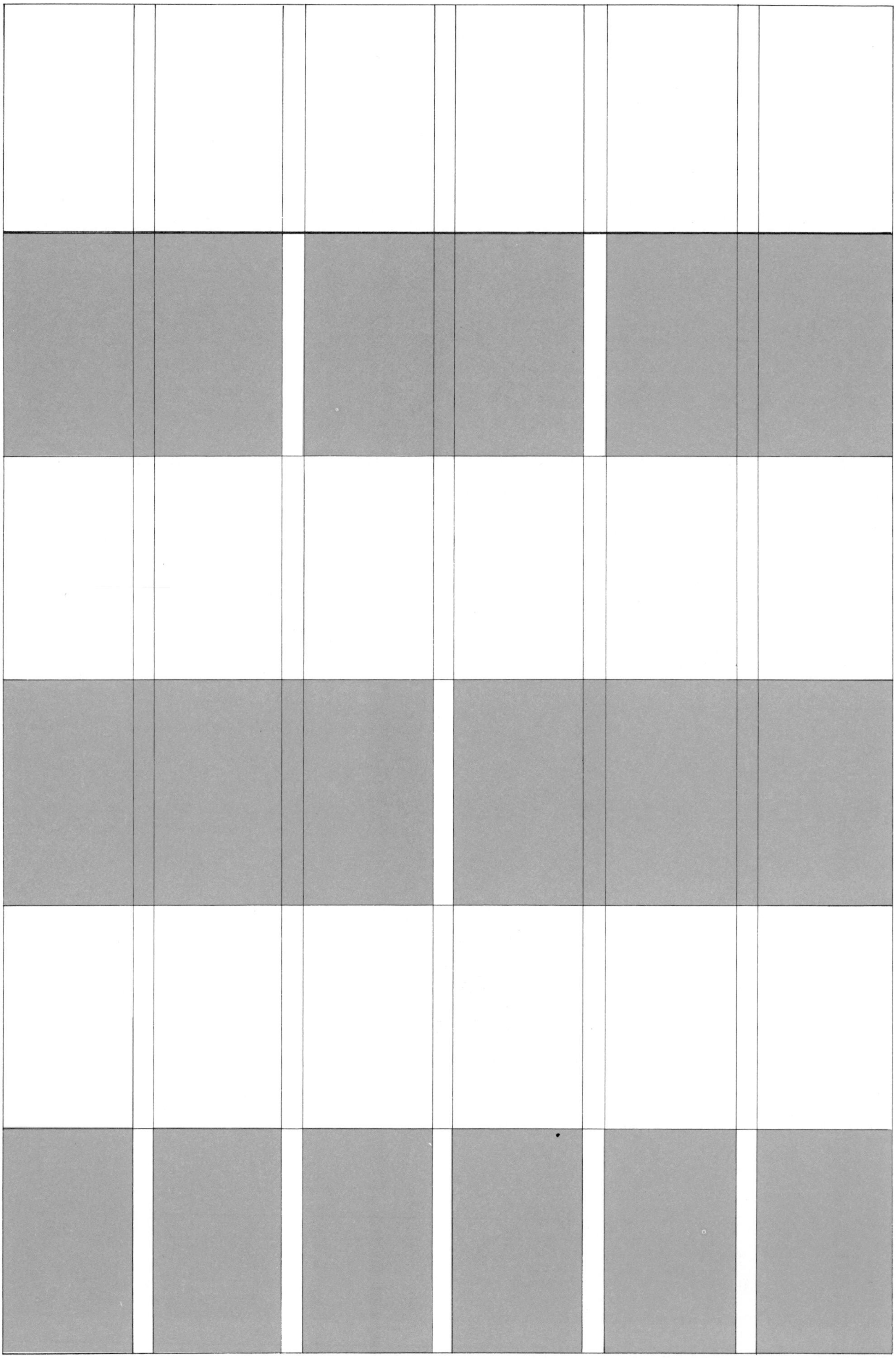

Magazines

This six-unit grid is designed to serve the needs of many different magazines working in the popular page sizes of approximately 8 × 11 inches (203 × 280mm). The grid provides the commonly used three-column makeup with 13-pica columns and an alternate two-column makeup with 20-pica columns. The horizontal divisions of this grid will accommodate ten lines of 11-on-12 type, twelve lines of 9-on-10, and fifteen lines of 7-on-8 point type.

The modern magazine, like the contemporary newspaper, has been undergoing intensive changes that have had a significant influence on its form and design. The visual emphasis that dominated magazines in the 1950s and 1960s and the fictional content of earlier periods have given way to a new emphasis on word content. The popular magazines of today rely more on information, reader service, and specialized appeals than on visual images or literary content.

By the 1970s many of the mass-circulation, general-interest magazines had ceased publication or shrunk in size. Most of the surviving magazines and the new ones that had rushed in to fill the gap are devoted to specialized interests—regional, demographic, or ideological—covering a multitude of in-home and outside subjects.

To understand the present situation and what lies ahead for publications it may be useful to trace the development of magazines in the past. In the 1920s, when graphic designers first became seriously involved in magazine formats, most publications were made up of highly structured pages that often consisted of unrelieved columns of type. Headlines were standardized and illustrations and borders filled whatever holes the text might provide.

By the end of the 1920s, the influence of the revolution in form that drew its freedom from the cubist, futurist, and dada movements and its new discipline from de Stijl and constructivism began to break the boundaries of the printed page. This approach brought a new freedom to page layout. Visual elements began to take on a dominant role. Bleed photographs, free-form illustrations, large areas of white space, and dramatic typography identified a magazine as modern. This trend continued into the 1960s when two influences began to again reshape the layout of magazine pages. A new emphasis on word content underscored the importance of typography, and a reaction to the excesses of visual dominance began to move layouts away from unbridled freedom of form and toward a new appreciation of order and structure. Typographic rules began to reappear in editorial layouts to emphasize the organization of the pages. The grid, which was originally used on technical and architectural journals, began to find its way into the design of a far wider range of publications.

Each year a growing number of publications are switching from hot-metal composition to one or another system of filmsetting, and today magazine headlines are rarely set in metal type. As magazines have become more specialized, so have their problems. This makes it difficult to generalize about the effects of the technical revolution on magazine design, but it is now clear that film is becoming the dominant material in publication production. It has expanded the designer's range of selection and added greatly increased flexibility to his typographic options. Together with these gains, however, there has been a corresponding loss in the imposed discipline of the metal form.

It is also difficult to make a precise measurement of the effect of these changes on design procedures because of a lack of uniformity in current working methods. Each magazine has its own way of dealing with editing, copy preparation, design, proofreading, and makeup. In addition, many publications have inherited their working methods from already abandoned printing technology, and each magazine's routine is influenced by its size, frequency, and editorial objectives. There are a few basic steps in the production process that are common to most magazines. The process begins with an understanding of the nature of the magazine and its editorial objectives together with an appreciation of the line of communication contained in a given article.

After allowing for the constraints and individual variations that exist between different magazines, the procedure from idea to finished pages will follow a pattern something like this: 1. a rough visual of the idea; 2. an accurate layout drawn to the exact dimensions of the page or spread; 3. type specifications, galley proof or printout, and corrections; 4. a rough paste-up for letterpress or a precise paste-up mechanical, including camera-ready typography for any other process; 5. a page lock-up for letterpress or a negative film assembly for offset or gravure; 6. a page proof or a printout of the page for final approval.

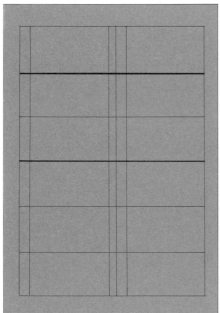

This is an example of the kind of magazine content that lends itself to computer-aided design and area composition. I designed the grid in 1972 for *Homelife*, a weekly magazine with a small format. The text was computer set and stored, and each week it was updated by the tape merger process. The grid made direct-film assembly possible and was planned for automated makeup.

It is easy to see that there is a duplication of effort in this series of steps, and it is here that the process may benefit from some modification. One way to simplify the process is to go directly from the layout and preliminary type corrections to film assembly, and it is obvious that the grid has real advantages in this method. When a layout is carefully planned in accordance with a workable grid, and when it is executed in a way that leaves no doubt about type positions and picture size and cropping, it is a simple matter for technicians to translate into final page form.

At this stage it is difficult to forecast the future course of magazine production technology, but it is becoming increasingly clear that whatever form it takes, the grid will serve as an increasingly important instrument in the design of magazines. It is also clear that no simple standardized grid can satisfy the specialized needs of all magazines. Many magazines have service content in the front and back pages, and it is this type of content that can easily be serviced by grids and may eventually lend itself to automated area composition with preplanned grids guiding technical assembly of text and visual elements. A fairly clear example of how this content can be applied to automated makeup is in the

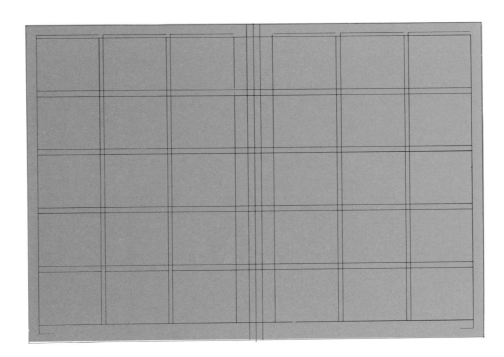

16/5   INDUSTRIAL DESIGN

Materials
Product planning
Product design
Packaging

Export and import:
design for foreign markets
AMA packaging show
Using steel in furniture

Published for industrial designers
and for executives throughout industry
who are concerned with product planning
and development, including product
design, materials specifications,
packaging, graphics and marketing.

June 1969, Volume 16, Number 5

6 In this issue

8 News — A report on the signage system developed by David Mellor for Britain's Ministry of Transport . . . Results of the 1969 British Poster Design Awards competition . . . . Who's doing what for whom.

29 Editorial

30 Sign language — The universal operator's symbols developed by Henry Dreyfuss Associates for John Deere and an important step toward an international symbol language.

34 Say "Ford" with a foreign accent — It's difficult to tell whether Ford's foreign models are the step-children or heirs apparent to the company's domestic cars.

38 For the American market — Quietly—since it will not be available in Europe—Alfa Romeo has introduced a fuel injection system for its export models.

40 You don't have to know the language — With offices in New York, Munich, Mexico and Tokyo, designer Albrecht Goertz talks about his own international design practice.

44 F.O.B. Milan — Not all of the products of the Gavina furniture factory are available here; some are sold only abroad by Knoll.

46 Shop rights — If a designer conceives an idea while working for someone else—and he is working in the general field of that idea—to whom does that idea belong?

48 Brazilian baroque — Damaz and Weigel's design for Banco do Brasil in Manhattan combines an elegant architectural statement with a functional banking space.

52 Design in action — Lighting fixtures from Germany and the first transistor-operated clock to be made in Italy are among this month's new designs.

58 Keep New York posted — Container Corporation of America has donated a series of posters to the city and will match anyone else's similar donation.

60 More on the elusive safety car — Until now, safety cars have been ugly ducklings, futurama style; Brock Stevens argues that this needn't be the case and that the limitation safety imposes can be used to the designer's advantage.

62 Materials guide #23 — Architect and designer Warren Platner is the author of this month's guide to working with steel in furniture design.

68 The AMA packaging show — Ed Kozlowski, package designer, describes the AMA show emphasizing new developments and their significance for the designer.

74 Packaging round-up — This month's selection includes highlights from the Alcoa student design awards program as well as in-use retail and industrial packaging.

78 Equipment and materials — The component and new equipment designs described here aid the designer by keeping him informed of the latest improvements.

80 Technical literature — Keyed to our computerized reader service cards, these catalogs, guides and fact sheets provide the know-how essential for professional competence.

86 Calendar

87 Reader Service cards

In July/August

Products especially designed for the needs of the handicapped will be examined in this forthcoming issue of INDUSTRIAL DESIGN. Work on design for the handicapped is well within the scope and abilities of the designer as is proven by the fact that he is the man the medical profession often turns to for new means of meeting the burden. And the industrial designer has been highly successful in this field where human factors play a large role in any design. While the focus of this special report will be on design for the handicapped, the whole field of medical design will be investigated. The subject of this month's designer: materials guide will be laminating various materials, such as paper, polyethylene, cellophane and vinyl, to aluminum foil for packaging applications. Award-winning student designs using aluminum, paper, paperboard, and corrugated for packaging will be the main feature in the July/August packaging section.

In September

The subject of this month's special report is appliance design. Perhaps the best known products of industrial design are the appliances used in most American kitchens today. Has the industrial designer met the human engineering demands of the housewife, or are most appliance designs just slight modifications of last year's models? What accounts for the success of the Braun line of small appliances which have had such an impact on the design of American models? Are Braun appliances successful simply because they presented a new face of design or because they represented significant breakthroughs in materials use and human engineering? These are some of the questions that will be answered—and next—in this forthcoming issue. Retail packaging displays will be the subject of the September packaging section along with a feature on the moral responsibility of the package designer.

Publisher: Charles E. Whitney
Executive Vice President
George Mc'. Whitney
Editor-in-Chief: J. Roger Guilfoyle
Design Direction: Massimo Vignelli
Art Assistant: Robert Winters
Associate Editor: Barbara J. Allen
Assistant Editor: Suzanne Slesin
Office Manager: Dennis B. Jones
Advertising Manager: Guy Vogée
Circulation Manager: Murray Sorauna
Production Manager: Ben P. Marchetto
West Coast Correspondent:
Judith Ransom Miller

Publication Offices
Whitney Publications, Inc.
18 East 50 Street, New York, N.Y. 10022
Charles E. Whitney, President and Treasurer
Jean McClellan Whitney, Vice President
Copyright 1969
Whitney Publications, Inc.
All rights reserved. The trademark "INDUSTRIAL DESIGN" is registered in the U.S. Patent Office

INDUSTRIAL DESIGN is published 10 times a year, combining Jan. Feb. and July/Aug. issues, at 10 McGovern Ave, Lancaster, Pa. 17604, by Whitney Publications, Inc. : Editorial and Executive Offices: 18 East 50 Street, New York, N.Y. 10022: Subscription Price $10 for one year, $18 for two years, $24 for three years in the United States. Possessions and Canada. Rates to countries of the Pan American Union are $12 for one year, $22 for two years, $30 for three years. Rates to all other countries are $14 for one year, $26 for two years, $36 for three years. Price per copy $1.50 in U.S.A., Possessions and Canada, $2 to all other countries. Second-class postage paid at Lancaster, Pa. 17604. All material submitted for publication is carefully evaluated by the editors. No material can be returned unless accompanied by a stamped, return envelope.

Member, American Business Press, Inc.   Member, Audit Bureau of Circulations   Member, Second Class Mail Publications, Inc.

Design in action

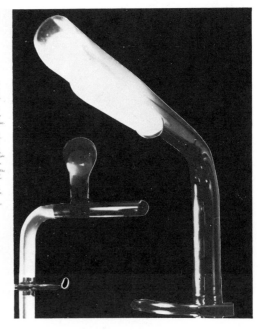

The simple three-unit grid for *Industrial Design* magazine (upper left) was designed by Massimo Vignelli. Note how the vertical and horizontal coordinates position the text areas on the contents page and the illustrations on the product pages (lower left). The bold contrasts of value and image size add impact to the simple and direct design.

broadcast or entertainment program listings. This content contains a fair amount of repeat material that is suitable for computer storage and retrieval. It also is made up of items that can be placed by standard instructions. In the future the controlled use of area composition for this content may well free the magazine designer to devote more of his time to the creative challenges of page design.

The design grid was originally used in magazines devoted to subjects like art, architecture, and design, where the modular approach was appropriate for both the subject matter and its presentation. Magazines like *Domus* in Italy, *Design* in England, *Du* in Switzerland, and *Industrial Design* in America were the proving ground of the magazine grid. For many years they have continued to demonstrate how the grid can bring a sense of proportion, order, and continuity to the modern magazine.

In other types of magazines, the grid has moved more slowly toward general acceptance. In my own designs for *Look* magazine, where I served as art director for nearly fifteen years, I resisted the grid because I found it inhibiting to the dramatic changes in form that I found essential to the

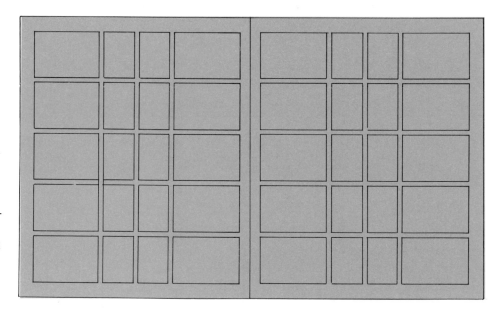

The grid reproduced on this page was also designed by Massimo Vignelli for a magazine of architectural criticism called *Oppositions*. This grid uses a different approach to the problem of two- and three-column makeup from the one on page 48.

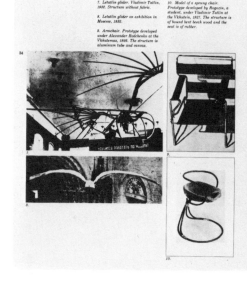

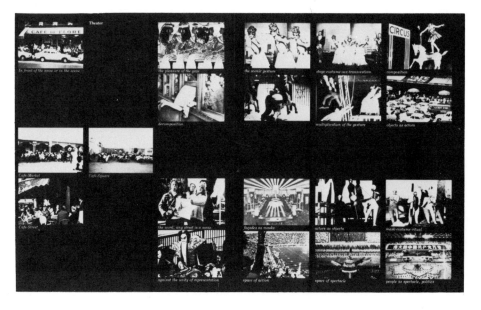

highly visual material with which I was working. Although I avoided a tightly structured system, I developed a sense of order—an imaginary grid—that played an increasingly important part in the division of space in my page designs.

In recent years I have worked as a design consultant on several different magazines and I have found the grid to be an essential tool in developing the style and personality of a magazine. In these situations I also found that the grid provided a unifying concept that guided the staff designers in the implementation of the format. These designers were then able to channel their own creative contributions toward a continuity of style and editorial presentation.

With the varied content of most magazines there are times when more than one grid may be needed to serve the format. Sometimes this is accomplished with separate makeup sheets, but, where possible, the different grids are superimposed or combined into a single framework. The most successful grids are designed to satisfy all of the requirements of the content. For example, a six-unit grid may never be used for six columns of type. In pairs, however, these units provide for a three-column makeup, and, in multiples of three, the same grid sets the framework for a two-column page (see page 48). The horizontal divisions can also be planned to work with different type sizes as well as variations in the treatment of visual material.

One of the most notable grids ever developed for magazine layout was the one that Willy Fleckhaus devised for *Twen* magazine in Germany in 1959. With this unique grid he designed some superb layouts using varied content over the decade of the 1960s. The grid was a twelve-unit grid (also called a twelve-line grid) and it was designed for a large page size—$10\frac{1}{2} \times 13\frac{1}{2}$ inches (267×343mm). The small dimension of the grid only gave a column width of about 4 picas and it was probably never used; but by combining the units, Fleckhaus had the option of working in a six-, four-, three-, or two-column typesetting. The horizontal divisions were coupled with nine divisions of the vertical space, creating a whole series of coordinates for the placement of visual matter and text units.

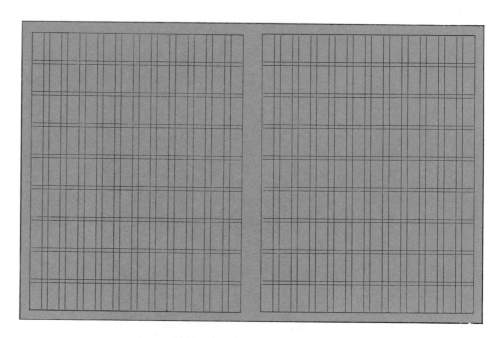

One of the most remarkable magazine grids is the twelve-unit grid designed by Willy Fleckhaus for *Twen* magazine in the early 1960s. This somewhat unorthodox grid introduced an almost unlimited series of options for column widths and pictorial cropping, but the secret of its success here was not so much its structure as the imagination with which it was used.

SCHULE DES CHARMES

Will Hopkins, who had worked with Fleckhaus on *Twen*, used the twelve-unit grid to design many effective spreads for *Look* magazine (above). Recently, he has adapted that grid to fit the smaller page size as his spread from *Wharton* magazine demonstrates at the left.

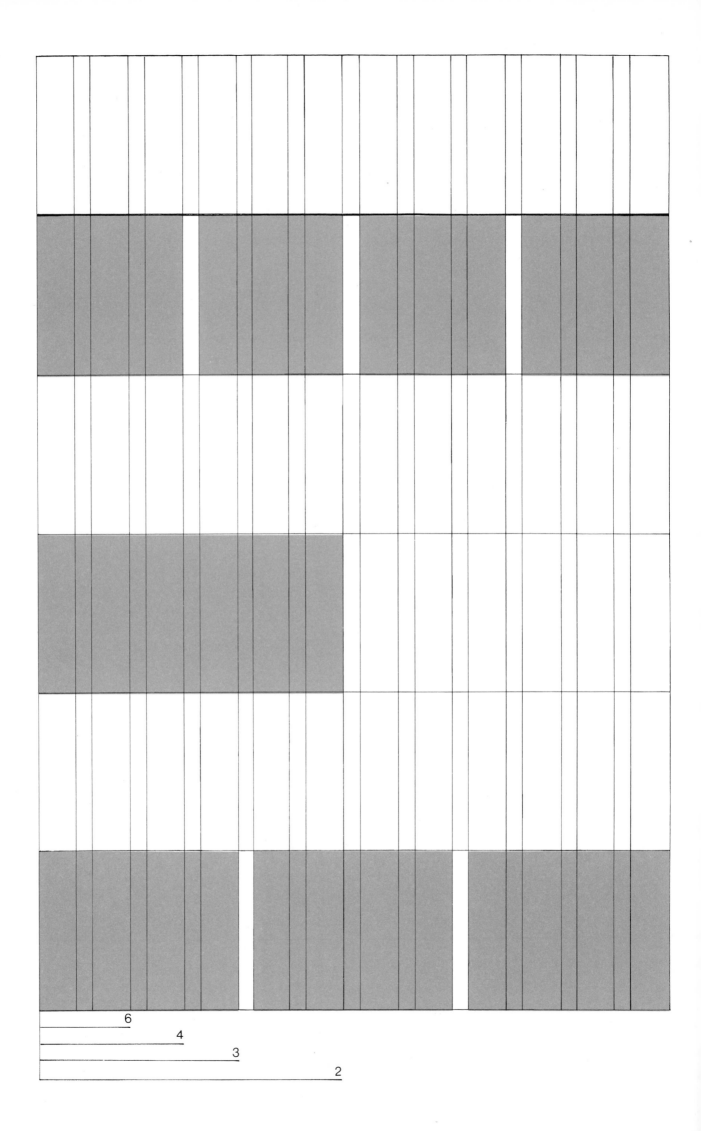

6

4

3

2

The grid reproduced at the left is a modification of the *Twen* grid for a smaller magazine. The shaded areas indicate three different column widths that the grid provides. Several other options exist. The horizontal divisions are planned to work with a variety of type sizes (see page 48), but this grid has also been used with squares as the detail from the grid below demonstrates.

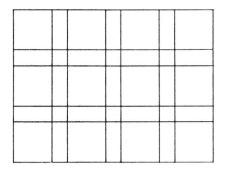

The complex grid (right) designed by Karl Gerstner for *Capital*, a Swiss magazine, also creates the option of two, three, four, and six columns, but it would be more difficult to work with than the grid shown on the facing page.

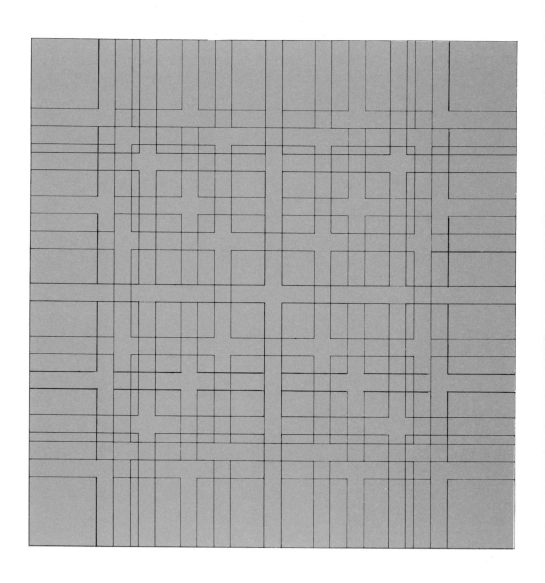

One of Willy Fleckhaus' design assistants was Will Hopkins, who later became my associate art director at *Look* magazine and who then became its art director in 1969. At *Look* Will Hopkins continued to work with a modification of the *Twen* grid, though he placed less emphasis on the horizontal divisions. His layouts are a further demonstration of the effectiveness of this design system, and in recent years he has adjusted this grid to serve the more popular small magazine format (see page 57).

An even more complex example of the multiple function grid is the one designed by Karl Gerstner for the

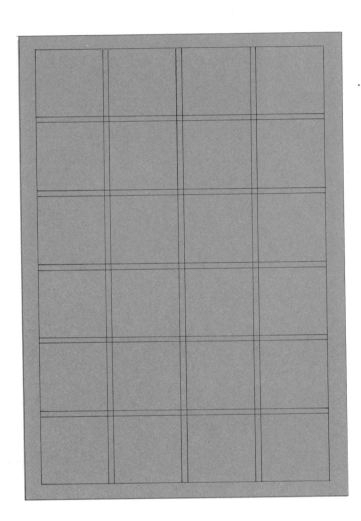

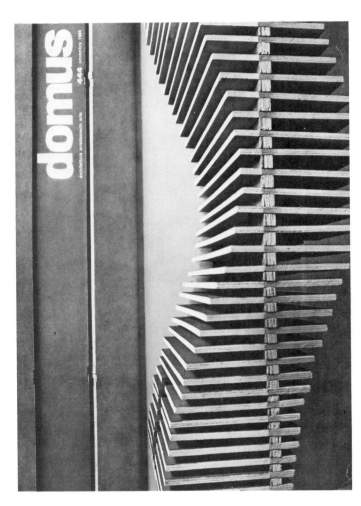

For many years the pages of *Domus*, an Italian magazine designed by Lisa Ponti and Giovanni Fraschioni, have been admired for the crispness of the design and the boldness of the visual display. These pages have been uniquely designed to place typographic and visual elements on the horizontal or vertical axis.

Swiss publication *Capital*. This is actually a six-column grid with a four-column grid superimposed (see page 59). This grid also gives an option of six, four, three, and two columns with an added option of the unusual five-column layout. This grid requires considerable study, and a designer would have to spend a great deal of time working with it before he could make free use of it in a creative sense.

At about the same time that Fleckhaus was designing his twelve-unit grid for *Twen* in Germany, Brian Grimbly was working out a similar grid for *Design* magazine in London. This grid was planned for a somewhat smaller page size—8¼ × 11¾ inches (210 × 297mm). This grid followed the more orthodox division of both dimensions equally to form 2½-pica squares separated by 1-pica spaces. A section

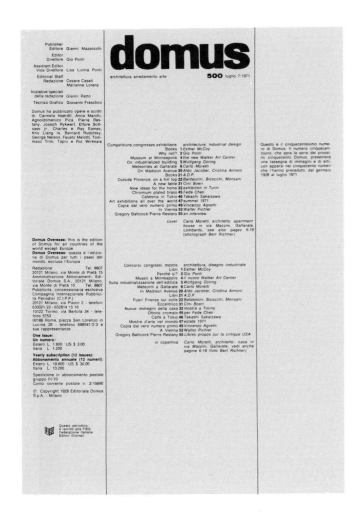

of this grid is reproduced on page 59. The uniformity of this grid has advantages from a design viewpoint, but it presents problems when different type sizes are used in the wide and narrow measures.

Perhaps a more typical magazine grid is the one designed by Massimo Vignelli for *Industrial Design*. This is a basic three-column grid with provision for some optional setting. It includes a careful division of the vertical space to provide for illustrations of many sizes and proportions and to produce a variety of layouts (see page 52).

For many years *Domus*, an Italian magazine devoted to architecture and design, worked with a grid that permitted the content to be placed horizontally across the spread or vertically if the magazine was turned to take advantage of the

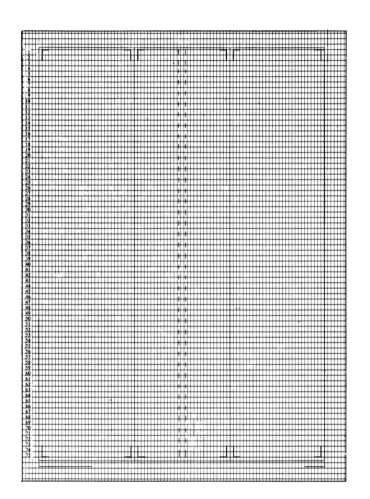
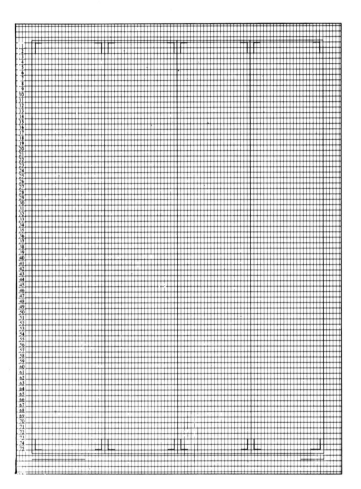

These grids, prepared for Walter Bernard's 1977 redesign of *Time* magazine, are not much more than makeup sheets, but they emphasize the technical precision required in the fast-moving makeup of a modern computerized publication.

upright shape.

Magazines devoted to news and current events have always required the kind of content organization that suggests modular design systems, but few of them have taken advantage of this opportunity. There have been a few notable exceptions. In 1974 Will Hopkins developed a twelve-unit grid system as part of the restyling of *L'Express*, a Paris-based news magazine. Three years later in 1977, *Time* magazine introduced a format that organized the content in a completely modular system, under the art direction of Walter Bernard, who had previously served as art director of *New York* magazine with design director Milton Glaser. Walter Bernard worked out a grid for the handling of the text and the visual content of *Time* that had a remarkable clarity and

These three- and four-column pages from the restyled version of *Time* magazine illustrate the way in which typographic rules can give a gridlike structure to modular magazine design.

continuity, but that also provided the flexibility necessary for variety and visual emphasis.

Anyone who has wondered where the old hairline divider rules of newspapers have gone needs only to examine some of the modern magazines. Since 1960 several publications have made use of these rules in one way or another. *Twen*, *New York*, and *Rolling Stone* were pioneers in the revival of the hairline rule, and these typographic dividers form a critical part of the new format of *Time* magazine, where they create a visible grid on the printed page.

The grid, like any other instrument in the design process, is not an absolute. It should be used with flexibility, and when necessary it should be modified or abandoned completely for a more workable solution. Generally, it is wise for a designer who has not worked with grids to begin with a simple form. He should never choose a framework that in any way contradicts his natural feeling toward layout or his personal style, but at the same time he should not be afraid to experiment or explore new areas of his own growth as a designer. As his experience grows, the enterprising designer may want to extend the geometry of his grids into more complex forms. Some magazine designers may elect to abandon all of the controls of the grid except for the simple demarcation of columns and margins. But most will find that there are advantages in the guidelines that more sophisticated grids offer, even though the constraints may sometimes have to be set aside for creative considerations.

A major virtue of the grid system is the discipline it imposes on the untrained designer. As a teacher of publication design, I have found that it is only when the student divides and analyzes the space he is working with that he is able to achieve a cohesive design solution. In a magazine design project the student is expected to prepare a flat plan for his publication consisting of a dozen or more spreads. While he is not required to use a grid in his final design, he is encouraged to prepare a tentative grid at this exploratory stage. The layouts for this flat plan are usually prepared in one-quarter or one-third scale, and when the exercise is completed most student designers have a concept of the total full-size magazine and a clear idea of how the grid can function in the design process.

3. books

egiptius de manu ysmahelitaꝛ: a qͥbꝫ
ꝓductus erat. Fuitꝙ dñs cu eo: et erat
uir i cuctis ꝓspere agẽs. Habitauitꝙ
iu domo dñi sui: qui optime nouerat
dñm esse cu eo: et oia que gereret ab eo
dirigi i manu illi⁹. Inuenitꝙ ioseph
graciã coram dño suo: ⁊ ministrabat
ei. A quo ꝓpositus omnibꝫ guberna
bat creditã sibi domũ: ⁊ uniuersa que
ei tradita fuerãt. Benedixitꝙ dñs do
mui egiptij ꝓpter ioseph: ⁊ multiplica
uit tam i edibus qͥ iu agris cunctam
ei⁹ sũbstantiã. Nec quicꝗ aliud noue
rat: nisi panẽ quo uescebat. Erat aũt
ioseph pulcra facie: et decorus aspectu.
Post multos itaꝗ dies· iniecit dña
oculos suos in ioseph: et ait. Dormi
mecũ. Qui nequaꝗ acquiescens operi
nephario: dixit ad eã. Ecce dñs meus
omnibus michi traditis: ignorat qͥd
habeat in domo sua: nec quicꝗ ẽ qd
non sit in mea potestate· uel nõ tradi
derit michi: preter te que uxor ei⁹ es.
Quõ ergo possũ hoc malũ facere: ⁊ pec
care i dñm meũ? Huiuscemodi uͤbis ꝑ
singulos dies loquebat: et mulier mo
lesta erat adolescenti: et ille recusabat
stuprũ. Accidit aũt quadã die ut in
traret ioseph domũ· et operis quippiã
absꝗ arbitris facere: ⁊ illa apꝓhensa
lacinia uestimenti ei⁹ diceret. Dormi
mecũ. Qui relicto i manu ei⁹ pallio
fugit: ⁊ egressus ẽ foras. Cũꝗ uidisset
mulier uestem in manibus suis: ⁊ se esse
contemptã: uocauit ad se homines dom⁹
sue: et ait ad eos. En introduxit uirũ
hebreũ: ut illuderet nobis. Ingressus
est ad me: ut coiret mecũ. Cumꝗ ego
succlamassem: ⁊ audisset uocem meã:
reliquit palliũ qd tenebam: ⁊ fugit fo
ras. In argumentũ ergo fidei· retentũ
palliũ ostendit marito reuertenti domũ·

et ait. Ingressus ẽ ad me seruus hebre⁹
quẽ adduxisti: ut illuderet michi. Cũꝗ
audisset me clamare: reliquit palliũ
qd tenebam: ⁊ fugit foras. His audi
tis dñs· et nimiũ credulus uerbis con
iugis· iratus est ualde: tradiditꝗ io
seph in carcerem ubi uincti regis custo
diebant: ⁊ erat ibi clausus. Fuit aũt
dñs cũ ioseph et misertus est illi⁹: ⁊ de
dit ei graciã in conspectu principis car
ceris. Qui tradidit in manu illi⁹ uni
uersos uinctos qui i custodia tenebãt:
et quidquid fiebat· sub ipo erat: nec no
uerat aliquid· cuctis ei creditis. Dñs
enͥ erat cũ illo: ⁊ oia opera ei⁹ dirigebat.

His itaꝗ gestis: accidit ut **Cᵽ xl**
ꝑpeccarent duo eunuchi· pincerna
regis egipti et pistor· dño suo. Iratus
ꝗ contra eos pharao· nam alter pin
cernis ꝑerat· alter pistoribꝫ: misit eos
in carcerem principis militũ· in quo
erat uinctus ⁊ ioseph. At custos carce
ris tradidit eos ioseph: qͥ et ministra
bat eis. Aliꝗntulũ tͣpis fluxerat: et illi
in custodia tenebant. Videruntꝗ ambo
somniũ nocte una: iuxta interptacio
nem congruã sibi. Ad quos cũ intro
isset ioseph mane· ⁊ uidisset eos tristes:
sciscitat⁹ ẽ dicens. Cur tristior ẽ hodie
solito facies uestra? Qui responderut.
Somniũ uidim⁹: et non est qui inter
ꝑetur nobis. Dixitꝗ ad eos ioseph.
Nũquid nõ dei ẽ interptacio? Referte
michi quid uideritis. Narrauit prior
ꝓpositus pincernarũ· somniũ suũ. Vi
debam coram me uitem in qua erant
tres ꝑagines crescere paulatim i gem
mas: ⁊ post flores uuas maturescere:
calicemꝗ pharaonis in manu mea.
Tuli ergo uuas ⁊ expressi i calicem quẽ
tenebam: ⁊ tradidi poculũ pharaoni.
Respondit ioseph. Hec est interpretaͣ

Books

A careful study of Johann Gutenberg's forty-two line bible, the first printed book, reveals guidelines that served as a primitive typographic grid. The reproduction at the left is from the vellum edition in the Pierpont Morgan Library.

The entire tradition and style of bookmaking was established in a comparatively short period—from the beginning of printing in 1454 to the close of the fifteenth century, only forty-six years later. This period of printing, which scholars call the "incunabulum" (cradle), saw the refinement of the Roman alphabet by early punch cutters like Nicolaus Jenson and Francesco Griffo into the form we now accept as classic. This period of history was also responsible for the production of a surprising number of volumes, including several that have been models for book designers for nearly 500 years. Among these books were *Eusebius* by Nicolaus Jenson in 1470, *Euclid* by Erhard Ratdolt in 1482, and *Poliphilus* printed by Aldus Manutius in 1499 with a typeface by Francesco Griffo. These books were all printed in Venice, and between them they contained most of the ideas of proportion, typographic spacing, and the placement of illustration that are still in vogue. Any one of them could serve as a guide for the contemporary designer of fine books.

If a designer looks carefully at some of the vellum sheets of Gutenberg's original forty-two-line bible completed in 1455, he will find traces of the grid on which he based the layout of his pages. These lines guided the positioning of the double columns of forty-two lines, controlled the margins, and located the folios and headings. This pattern of lines was inspired in part by the guidelines of inscribed Gothic manuscripts and in part by the rigid wooden frames and metal type that made up Gutenberg's primitive forms.

A few years after the end of the period identified as "incunabula," another book was published that was destined to have an influence on the form of the printed page. This book was called *De Divina Proportione* (see page 10). It was written by Fra Luca Pacioli, illustrated by Leonardo da Vinci, and it was more noted for its content than for its contribution to the bookmaker's art. Its revival of interest in classic proportion and its golden section was to have an influence on the continuing search for perfection among book designers from Geofroy Tory to Jan Tschichold.

For most all-text pages of contemporary books a simple concern for reading pleasure, an awareness of

These early pages from the *Poliphilus*, printed at the close of the fifteenth century, still stand as models for book design. Published by Aldus Manutius, it uses a type designed by Francesco Griffo. These pages are from the British Library Collection.

proportion, and a straightforward margin scheme normally dictate a grid that is not much more complex than were the guidelines for type placement in Gutenberg's day.

There is an important printing characteristic that has influenced grid patterns since the earliest printed pages. The heavy impression of letterpress printing often created a strike-through that was clearly visible on the verso of a sheet. To cover this the type was positioned on both sides of a page in a matching format. This created a mirror image on a book spread with equal facing inner and outer margins. In modern printing this problem still exists, but in a slightly different way. While strike-through is rarely a problem in modern presswork, show-through is. When lightweight

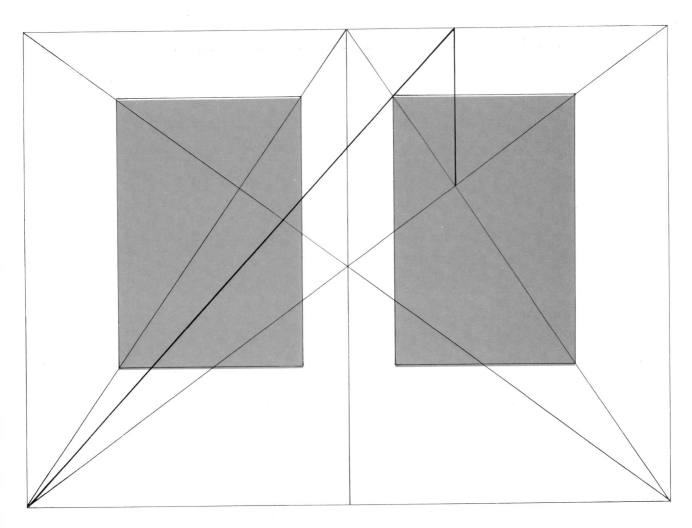

This diagram illustrates one of many ways that the classic proportions of the printed page can be determined. The resulting margins may be overly generous for most readers and for most contemporary book production.

papers are used the mirror layout has a major functional advantage.

The advent of coated paper and halftone surfaces with high opacity solved the problems of show-through, and this in turn led to greater freedom in layout and a more asymmetrical form. These new forms became particularly valuable when the layout of pictorial material was coupled with the placement of text. When running text is positioned on the right-hand side of both pages the layout normally presents better opportunities for picture placement (the layout of this book is a case in point).

In working out even the simplest grid most book designers begin with a flat plan consisting of about a dozen

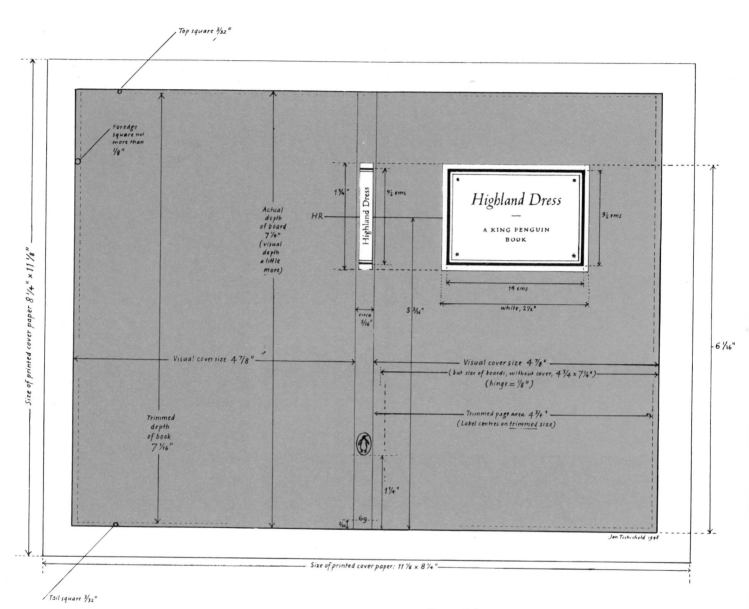

One of the precise typographic grids created by Jan Tschichold to control the design and production of Penguin Books is shown with his detailed instructions above. The design is characteristic of the formal and traditional approach found in Tschichold's later work.

critical spreads. The flat plan will usually be prepared in about one-quarter scale. The spreads will be executed either as thumbnail sketches or as rough paste-ups of halftones clipped from available sources and combined with rendered indications of type matter. The flat plan will usually include a title page, most of the front matter, and several typical spreads. In preparing a flat plan the designer should also concern himself with ideas for the binding and endpapers. Unfortunately, many publishers treat the book jacket as a separate entity, often using different designers for the book and its more advertising-oriented exterior. But, where possible, a better book will result when the total design is coordinated at an early stage of the design process.

In the advance planning stage the designer will also concern himself with the specific problems of the book's typography—the special demands of poetry and drama; the amount of text and its relation to type size and columns; the need for subheadings, tabular matter, diagrams, and listings. Behind the simplest grid there is often a complex process of analysis. Without the sketch layouts of a preliminary flat plan that tests the grid against the variations of content, it may become distorted by the many conditions it will be exposed to in the completion of the typographic design.

The classic page proportion is generally accepted as 2:3 with an equivalent, but somewhat smaller, rectangle for the text. The inside margin is one-half of the outside margin, and the top margin is half the size of the base margin. There are several methods of positioning the type within the page. One of the most commonly used is the diagram reproduced on page 69. Its origin is obscure, but it was rediscovered by van de Graaf and has been widely used by contemporary designers like Jan Tschichold. The proportion of 2:3 is close to, but not precisely equal to, the golden section, which is 0.618:1.

The modern book designer will find classic proportion interesting, but will be more inclined to use his own judgement in working out the format of his pages. He will usually rely on his own innate sense of proportion, his design experience, and the conditions and the constraints of the

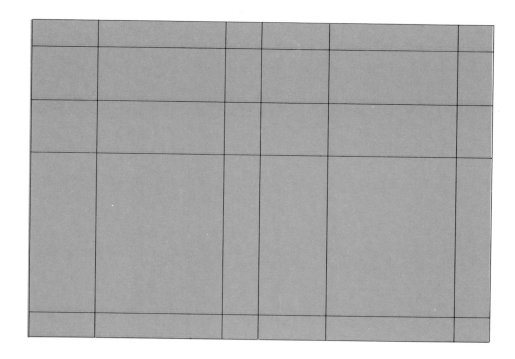

Bradbury Thompson's typographic grid (right) and the spreads on the facing page from an American Institute of Graphic Arts publication demonstrate how a simple grid can give form and structure to a book.

project in hand. Pleasant as traditional book margins are, they are often ill suited to either the economics of modern publishing or the habits and expectations of contemporary readers. It is even possible that classic margins were based on the needed space for the scribe's hands as much as they were selected for their divine proportion.

In magazines and newspapers designers nearly always work within the set sizes of established format. The book designer, on the other hand, will often, but not always, have the right to select the size and shape of his pages. He will also have a unique concern with the thickness and weight of the resulting volume and to this extent his design will become three-dimensional. The choice of size is not always the designer's prerogative. If the book is part of a series, a predetermined size may be indicated, and sometimes merchandising problems and economic considerations will determine the size and even the weight of a book.

Pocket books are an example of the ultimate constraints placed on a book designer. This important category of books has a standard size of 4⅜ × 7 inches (110 × 180mm), with only minor variations, in the proportion of

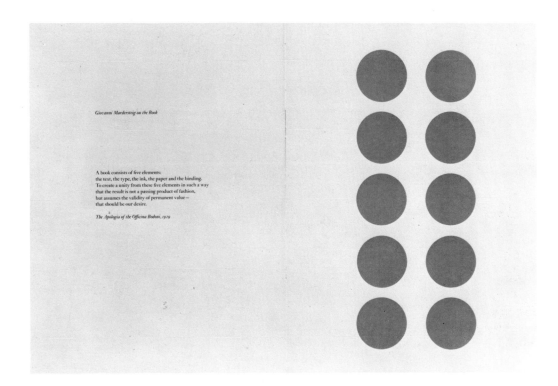

Giovanni Mardersteig on the Book

A book consists of five elements:
the text, the type, the ink, the paper and the binding.
To create a unity from these five elements in such a way
that the result is not a passing product of fashion,
but assumes the validity of permanent value —
that should be our desire.

The Apologia of the Officina Bodoni, 1929

The Fifty Books 1968

John Fillion

20 Notes by: Dorothy Cameron.
Publisher: The Martlet Press Ltd., Toronto.
Designer: Allan Fleming.
Art Director: Allan Fleming.
Photographer: John Reeves.
Format: 9½ by 12¾; 30 pages; edition of 2,500; price $19.00.
Composition: Torino, 30 on 38,
by Cooper & Beatty Ltd.
Presswork: Offset by Herzig-Somerville Ltd.,
on Consolidated Durado Offset dull coated,
supplied by Fine Papers Ltd.
Binding: Hamilton Ruling and Bindery Services Ltd.,
in Holliston Sailcloth,
supplied by Whyte-Hooke Papers.
Slipcase in Holliston Sailcloth.

The American Institute of Graphic Arts

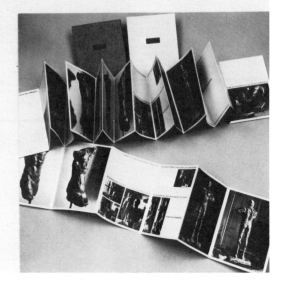

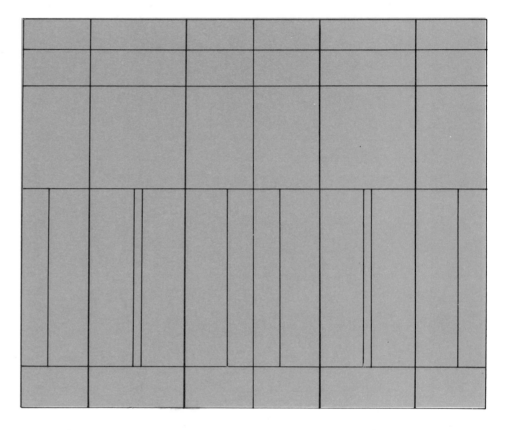

Another book grid designed by Bradbury Thompson for a collection of stories by Edgar Allan Poe. provided lines for the unique central axis of the typography.

3:5. This is a reasonably pleasant proportion, but a somewhat better proportion exists in French pocket books that are narrower in relation to their height and more nearly approximate the golden rectangle. With all the limitations that pocket books impose on the designer there have been some notable exceptions to the poor typography of most of these books. Jan Tschichold set a style for Penguin Books in England that resulted in clear and lucid typography, and the French book designers, with a long tradition of designing novels in small formats, still treat this page size with considerable respect.

The contemporary book serves many and varied purposes that influence the structure of grids and the shape of their design. Textbooks and educational books serve an expanding knowledge explosion that demands new visual treatment and new forms in bookmaking. Books published in a series must often work with a common grid or a grid adapted to serve an overall style, while also providing for the

The design of the spreads for Poe's *The Black Cat* effectively combines symmetrical elements within an asymmetrical framework.

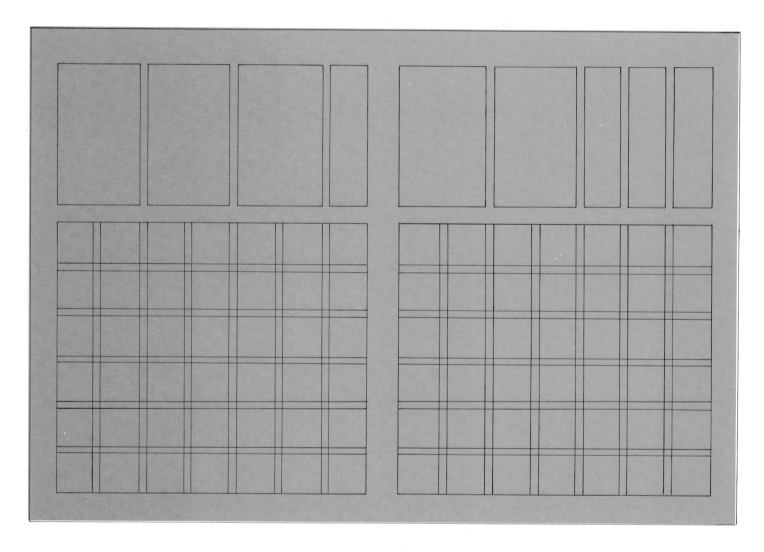

Ed Day, design director of Mitchell Beasley in London, designed this grid (above) to provide a master plan for a group of encyclopedias. The grid guided the creation of nearly 2000 pages with 11,000 color illustrations of widely varied content. The pages on the right are from the *Random House Encyclopedia*.

special needs of a given volume. Encyclopedias need grids that are rigid enough to keep the content organized and clear, but flexible enough to allow for widely varied visual material. Reference books in general need to be planned to take advantage of the storage and retrieval function of computerized composition, while providing for updating and modification with a minimum of resetting.

It is impossible in a study of this dimension to cover all of the aspects of book design, but no examination of the grid as a design instrument can be complete without an examination of some of the technical developments that may determine its future.

The classification of fish

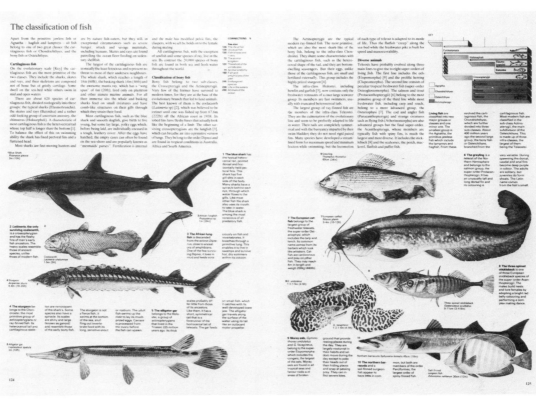

The anatomy of birds

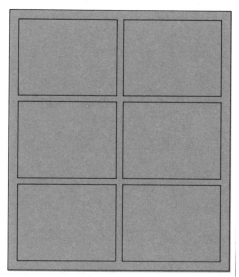

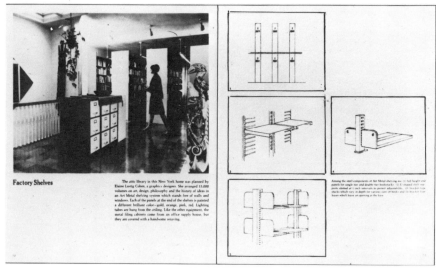

Factory Shelves

The simple grid (above) was designed by Lou Silverstein of the *New York Times* for a book about built-in furniture, consisting of diagrams, photographs, and short copy.

Hermann Zapf, one of the world's foremost designers of typefaces and books, had this to say about contemporary bookmaking in *Homage to the Book*: "The time is not far off when the manuscript will be put into a reading machine which, via a computer, produces the information necessary for book production on paper or magnetic tape. The computer will also be programmed to correct automatically . . . check the logic of thoughts . . . and even translate a complete work into a foreign language. The automated machine works to the programmed instructions fed into it, putting in running heads, chapter headings, folios, captions, and subtitles . . . performing other typographic chores. In this electronic future, the responsibility of the book designer will be even heavier. No longer will he be an unnecessary cost factor; he will direct the whole orchestra in which any false note means additional cost and loss of time."

These are not mere idle thoughts, but a recognition of the growing need for book publishing to examine current economic pressure in terms of future technological possibilities. Much of the hardware for this revolution is already beyond the prototype stage and the software is in research and development. Hermann Zapf and Aaron Burns, who is president of the International Typeface Corporation, have

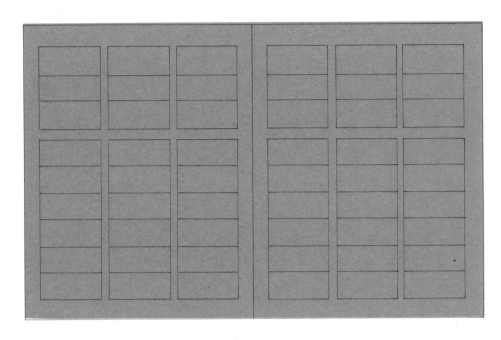

The grid at the right was designed for my recent book *Layout: the design of the printed page*. The basic grid structure not only guides the placement of varied word and visual content, but becomes a major force in the design of the book jacket.

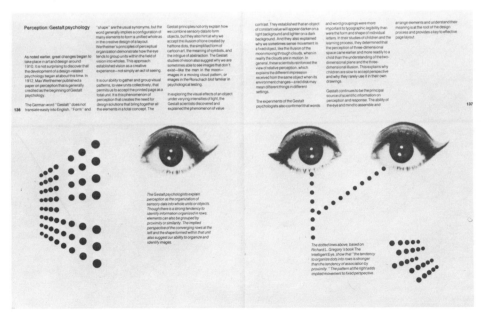

recently joined forces to set up a new company to supply the grids for automated area composition. The firm is called Design Processing International and its objective is to bring the talents of qualified designers to bear on the development of design structures, and overcome the technical limitations of computerized systems with a high standard of design.

There is no reason why book design should go on indefinitely with multiple proofs, piecemeal corrections, and pasted bits and pieces that mark the pattern of contemporary bookmaking. A properly planned grid with appropriate encoded specifications should be able to guide most trade books through a properly equipped photocomposition terminal and return the printouts in completely paginated form. Authors alterations, corrections, and typographic refinements could be incorporated automatically and almost instantaneously with automatic readjustment of pages to produce a complete revision.

For most publishers there are many questions to be answered and many problems to be overcome before they are ready for a full commitment to automated makeup. How much of the custom-made and handcrafted effect is a publisher willing to sacrifice? How will he weigh the economic advantages against his natural preference for more casual procedures? And finally, can he afford the capital investment that the new technology requires?

Whether book publishing goes all the way to embrace the full-scale automation that Hermann Zapf envisioned or merely extends its involvement into available systems, the grid will provide an important framework for future publishing. Whether it provides the simple skeleton for typographic clothing as it did in Gutenberg's time or whether it provides the base for a complex word processing and informational system of the twentieth century, the grid will be an important instrument in guiding the designer's concept through increasingly complex production processes.

Technical appendix

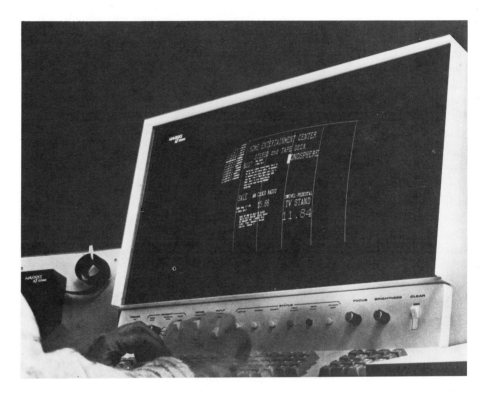

A complete typographic layout can be currently constructed with purely electronic controls and without benefit of markup or paste-up on units like the Harris 2200 Visual Display Terminal shown at the right. This equipment is currently being used for newspaper advertising composition, and it foreshadows a new generation of sophisticated terminals that will bring area composition to design.

In 1950 Jan Tschichold, a pioneer modern typographic designer and book stylist, began his treatise on book design by regretting the passing "of a world in which printer and publisher were one and the same person" and where all of the functions of bookmaking could be completed under the same roof. Though we left single-person publishing behind some centuries back, we are not far from the day when many of the functions of bookmaking that were so fragmented in the 1950s will come together again.

Even now it is possible for an author's manuscript typed in OCR (optical character recognition) readable letters to be directly scanned for typesetting without special keyboarding. From here it can be translated into tape, edited on CRT (cathode ray tube) screens and processed into columns of text. Without the need for intermediate printouts, this material can then be assembled in position on the page based on a prior layout or by manipulation on a VDT (video display terminal). At this point other elements of the layout are also incorporated, including display typography, line art, and screened halftones. The complete film assembly can then be printed out in page form for final approval and prepared for the transfer to printing plates. It is then possible to complete the printing, folding, collating, binding, addressing, and even mailing all in one continuous operation.

The part of this procedure that involves design systems and grids is primarily the point of assembly. Precisely how this will be handled is not yet completely clear, and it will certainly vary with the type of publication. In the case of the newspaper, the page makeup will probably involve a modular grid and a CRT, with the editor placing the elements in position in accordance with editorial needs and a designer's grid.

In the design of magazines the art director may manipulate his own arrangement in very much the same manner as he assembles a paste-up layout, but with the added advantage of the ability to instantaneously move elements, enlarge or reduce them, and exchange them for other available material. While this free play with space represents an interesting exercise, it is important that it be done in connection with a set module or a fairly firm concept.

In the 1960s *Life* magazine developed an instrument they called a layout machine, which provided an advance proving ground for this approach to design. This machine was basically a photomechanical instrument without any direct connection to production procedures. In fact, it had just enough built-in distortion to make it impractical as a guide to photoengravers and platemakers. But perhaps its greatest weakness was the difficulty the *Life* designers had in working with it, and, although its lessons were not final, it hinted that even more sophisticated area composition machines may be counterproductive in most magazine design.

Most of the major developments in computerized typography, editing, and layout have been inspired by the

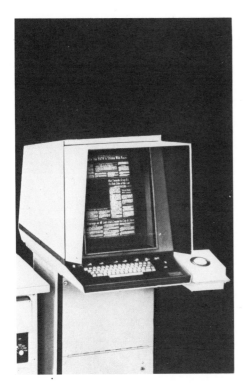

The System Five Page View Terminal by Mergenthaler Linotype Company (above) is similar to a battery of sixteen units that will control the makeup of the *New York Daily News*. These terminals bring to page design the frightening prospect of an automated system, where the console operator can visualize the page, experiment with alternate layouts, zoom in to change sizes, and sit back while the terminal produces a complete page in about 22 seconds.

needs of newspapers. In the years after World War II the graphic production costs began to soar out of control, and, once an accommodation was possible with the unions, major newspapers began to install computerized systems. These installations were complicated because of the volume and high-speed requirements, and they were often extremely expensive.

The dominance of newspapers in this development stage turned out to be a mixed blessing. On the positive side the technical knowledge gained in the process began to spin off new low-cost, high-quality, and versatile systems capable of serving small newspapers, magazines, and book publishers. Today it is possible for a small publisher to install a direct-entry photocomposition unit with storage and retrieval capability, as well as full correction potential, for a reasonable expenditure (under twenty thousand dollars at this writing). A single keyboard operator can handle the text and headline requirements of an average monthly magazine with time to spare when using this equipment.

Some other contributions of the pioneer efforts of newspapers in computer-aided reproduction have been less fortunate. The press's traditional low regard for typographic refinement and the low priority given to design considerations by the press have compromised quality and may have set back progress toward high-standard automated composition and makeup.

All recent technical developments have had a bearing on design, but the most important breakthrough has been in the introduction of automated area composition terminals. Currently, there are several machines capable of delivering full film assembly of all typographic elements within a 9- × 12-inch (229- × 305mm) rectangle. Several manufacturers are adding screened halftone images to these areas. New terminals capable of delivering full-size newspaper pages are well along the research and development line and tabloid-size units are already in use. Most of these terminals are based on the manipulation of images on a cathode ray tube (CRT), where a superimposed grid can assist the operator, but a new group of machines will be able to prepare complete film assemblies based on a selection of existing formats or grids. It is in this last development that design will play a principal role and it is to satisfy this role that new companies and units like Design Processing International are being formed. This company (see page 78) has been set up by Aaron Burns and Hermann Zapf to form a link between design and technology. While the creation of these grids presents an interesting challenge to the publication designer, they will not replace the creative ideas that add variety and distinction to the printed page.

Several hundred area composition machines are already in use and it is estimated that there will be over 200 of the large-size units capable of handling a full-size newspaper page by 1981. As in most cases of technological innovation, there are clear indications that the hardware (machine) will have a large lead on the software (talent and ideas).

Lou Silverstein, an award-winning design director of the *New York Times* and now its assistant managing editor, has had a unique close-up view of the promises and problems of the new technology. He believes that the "role of the art director in newspapers is being enhanced by the parallel track of technological change" and the shifts in editorial emphasis brought about by changing markets and "accelerated visual phenomena." He holds that this challenge will be handled "with a gradual movement of responsibility from someone called makeup editor to someone called art director, with a revamping of the role of picture editor in relation to art direction . . . as we wait to see who will push the technological button."

For magazines and books the waiting time for both hardware and software will be somewhat longer than for newspapers, but some of the work being done in the early stages suggests that when these systems are developed they will have an even closer link to design and modular systems and will place an even greater emphasis on the grid as a key to effective presentation.

Glossary of computer terminology

Many graphic designers in the publication field resist computerized composition and technical innovation because of their inability to cope with the surrounding language barrier. In the glossary that follows an attempt has been made to define some of the most frequently encountered terms in relatively simple language. In this fast-changing field no list can be complete, nor can it overcome all of the confusion that has resulted from casual and sometimes careless usage.

Area composition: Most cold-type composition is delivered in a single column printout similar to the galley proof of metal typesetting. Recently, there has been an effort to combine text elements, headlines and other illustrative and graphic content in a single printout that positions the material in a complete layout in accordance with manipulation on a CRT scanner or by the guidance of a programmed grid. This is also referred to as "automated makeup" or "modular area composition."

CAD—computer-aided design: The application of the computer to the analysis and processing of design data and the use of the computer as a manipulator of graphic material.

Cold-type composition: This is perhaps the only phrase that accurately covers the wide range of new typesetting methods available to the graphic designer. (See: Computerized composition, photocomposition or filmsetting, direct-entry typesetters, VDT, and typewriter composition.)

Computer: An information processor with the following characteristics: 1. it can receive and store large quantities of data in many forms; 2. it can operate on this data according to rules determined by the operator; 3. it can deliver data in mathematical, alphabetical, graphic, or other forms; 4. it can be programmed to select the data and process it in different ways and varying sequences.

Computerized composition (Computer composition): Though most cold typesetting machines use some computer aid, this phrase most accurately describes those systems that generate letters by electronic, rather than direct photographic, means.

CRT—cathode ray tube: An electronic tube that can be used to produce images for correction or editing. Also a tube used for exposure of letter-forming elements on film.

Direct-entry typesetters: A single-unit system with direct transmission from keyboard to typographic printout. Direct-entry units are compact and comparatively easy to operate, but they are slower and less sophisticated than units using perforated or magnetic tape.

Disk: A circular image-carrier of negative type fonts. Also (floppy disk), a method of storing and retrieving data in some systems.

GIGO: A somewhat irreverent term invented by pioneer computer operators to define the natural limits of the medium. It stands for "garbage in, garbage out" and emphasizes that results can never be better than the data on which they are based.

Grid: In this book the word "grid" refers to the drawn pattern of lines and coordinates that the designer uses as a framework for a design and its translation into printed form. To avoid confusion it should be pointed out that in photocomposition it also refers to a rectangular carrier of a negative type font that is used in some systems.

Hyphenation: Perhaps the most difficult problem in cold-type composition when justified lines are called for. It is usually solved by one of the following methods: 1. By the keyboard operator when the copy is set line-for-line on an on-line or direct-entry machine; 2. It is controlled by an operator using a CRT when continuous tape is fed into a console for setting; 3. It is handled automatically through stored information on syllable structure, which produces the proper hyphenated word breaks when the type lines are divided on an off-line system.

Line feed: A filmsetting term that describes the distance between the base of one line and the base of the following line. It takes the place of the term "leading" in hot-type composition. It is also called "line-spacing."

Line printer: A high-speed tape-activated machine that produces a printout for editing and proofreading purposes. It is usually set in a computer style of lettering rather than the actual typeface.

Menu: A catalogue of the optional grids (layout solutions) prepared for modular area composition.

On-line and off-line: Terms used to differentiate the direct-input machines that act directly from keyboard to setting (on-line) from the ones that act indirectly with the keyboard preparing tape for a separate feed into a console (off-line).

OCR—optical character recognition: Machine identification of letters from a special typewriter by optical methods. This system makes it possible to handle computer input without keyboard intervention.

Photocomposition or filmsetting: Any of the cold-type methods that produce letters by photographic means. These include most of the direct-input units, as well as many of the tape-generated consoles. These terms also cover a range of photo-mechanical units that specialize in the preparation of display type.

Printout: The end product in filmsetting that takes the place of the proof in hot-type composition. The printout can take many forms. It can be in the form of typewriterlike characters from a line-printer for proofreading or in the specified typeface on film or paper. It can be right-reading or left-reading and it can be negative or positive.

Tape: Many typesetting keyboards produce either punched tape (with encoded copy indicated by punched holes) or magnetic tape (with the same information represented by magnetic impulses). When this tape is run without line break indications it is sometimes called "idiot tape."

Tape merger: A fast and efficient method of incorporating typographic corrections and authors' alterations. The changes and line identifications are encoded on a new tape. This tape is run through a merging unit with the original uncorrected tape to create a third tape, which in turn generates a fully revised printout. A somewhat similar procedure is possible when the information is stored on disks. Both methods avoid piecemeal paste-up or wasteful resetting.

Typewriter composition: This typesetting method (sometimes referred to as "strike-on") grew out of the proportional typewriter and is most commonly identified with the IBM system. Though it is a relatively slow process, its low cost and simplicity of operation has made it a popular do-it-yourself method of typesetting. Newer and more sophisticated applications have combined tape with high-speed automated typewriters.

VDT—visual display terminal: A CRT that displays text as it is being set or after setting on a tape input for editing and correcting purposes. An adaptation of the VDT forms an essential part of most area composition systems.

Word processing: A term that defines the office functions of transcription, duplication, storage, and retrieval in an office as against a printing establishment. Some of the equipment is similar to that used in simple filmsetting operations.

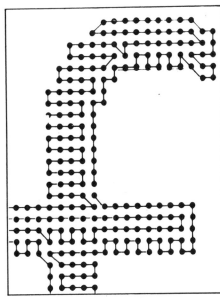

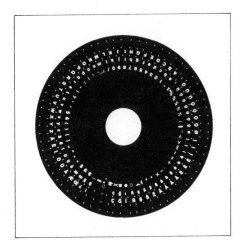

There are three ways that a letter can be formed in cold typesetting. It can be struck on as in the IBM type (above), it can be formed electronically (right), or it can take its shape through direct photographic exposure (far right).

Acknowledgments

When I began my research on this book about grids I soon discovered that there is remarkably little published documentation. From the start, it was clear that the main source of information would have to be gleaned from interviews and an examination of the work being done in this comparatively new field of design. I am particularly grateful to Paul Rand for his comments and guidance on this often complex subject and to Massimo Vignelli for making his extensive file of grid-oriented design available to me.

In exploring the relatively uncharted area of computer technology I am indebted to Edward Gottschall, Director of Information at the International Typeface Corporation, for the material he provided me with and the access to his list of sources in the fast-changing aspect of computer-aided design. I am also grateful to Professor Bruce Archer, head of Design Research at the Royal College of Art, for his assistance with the semantics of the new technology and his comments and additions to the "Glossary of Computer Terminology."

It would have been impossible to develop the sections on newspaper, magazine, and book design without the accumulated knowledge of all of the designers who have contributed to the mainstream of visual presentation. I would like to single out a few designers with particular thanks for their contributions: Louis Silverstein of the *New York Times*, Paul Back of *Newsday*, Edwin Taylor of the *London Sunday Times*, and Frank Ariss of the *Minneapolis Tribune* on newspapers; Willy Fleckhaus, Will Hopkins, and Walter Bernard on magazines; and Hermann Zapf, Bradbury Thompson, and Ed Day on books.

One of my principal sources of information on proportion and form was the vast collection of works available in the reading room of the British Museum. Another valuable source of published information on contemporary graphic design and technology was the extensive collection of books and periodicals in the library and the Learning Resources Center of the London College of Printing.

Finally, I would like to acknowledge the valuable editorial assistance of Nancy Newman Green, the Editor-in-Chief at Van Nostrand Reinhold, who also served as editor of my first book, *Publication Design*, and Susan Rosenthal, who edited this book. I would also like to express special thanks to my wife, Regina, for her patience and for the suggestions that helped me clarify my views on design, and to my daughter, Susan, whose early editing of the text contributed to its clarity as well as its accuracy.

Bibliography

Design:

Craig, James. *Production for the Graphic Designer*. New York: Watson-Guptill Publications, 1974.

Hofmann, Armin. *Graphic Design Manual*. New York: Van Nostrand Reinhold Company, 1965.

Hurlburt, Allen. *Layout: the Design of the Printed Page*. New York: Watson-Guptill Publications, 1977.

Müller-Brockmann, Josef. *The Graphic Artist and His Design Problems*. New York: Hastings House, Publishers, Inc., 1961.

Rand, Paul. *Thoughts on Design*. New York: Van Nostrand Reinhold Company, 1971.

Ruegg, Ruedi and Frohlich, Godi. *Basic Typography: Handbook of Technique and Design*. New York: Hastings House, Publishers, 1972.

Swann, Cal. *Techniques of Typography*. New York: Watson-Guptill Publications, 1969.

Proportion:

Gerstner, Karl. *Designing Programmes*. London: Tiranti, 1964.

Ghyka, Matila. *A Practical Guide to Geometric Composition and Design*. London: Tiranti, 1952.

Hambidge, Jay. *Elements of Dynamic Symmetry*. New Haven: Yale University Press, 1920.

Kepes, Gyorgy. *Module, Proportion, Symmetry, Rhythm*. New York: George Braziller, Inc., 1966.

Newspapers:

Evans, Harold. *Editing and Design—Book 5—Newspaper Design*. London: William Heinemann, Ltd., 1976.

Hutt, Allen. *The Changing Newspaper*. London: Gordon Fraser, 1973.

Magazines:

Hurlburt, Allen. *Publication Design*. New York: Van Nostrand Reinhold Company, 1976.

McLean, Ruari. *Magazine Design*. London: Oxford University Press, Inc., 1969.

Books:

Blumenthal, Joseph. *Art of the Printed Book*. New York: Pierpont Morgan Library, 1973.

Tschichold, Jan. *Designing Books*. New York: Wittenborn Schultz, no date.

Wilson, Adrian. *The Design of Books*. New York: Van Nostrand Reinhold Company, 1967.

Index

advertisements, 20–21, 26, 28
  computer composition of, 81
  in tabloids, 36
Aicher, Otl, 24–25
alphabet, 9, 24–25, 28
  history of printing and, 67
American Institute of Graphic Arts,
  73
annual reports, 18–19, 26
architecture:
  Japanese, 12
  the *Modulor*, 15–16
  perspective, 9
Ariss, Frank, 40–45
automated area composition
  terminals, 83

Back, Paul, 35
Bernard, Walter, 62–63
Bible, 66–67
Black Cat, The (Poe), 75
books, 66–80
  classic page proportion, 69,
   71–72
  computers for production of,
   78–80, 84
  encyclopedias, 76–77
  flat plan, 69–71
  grids for, 72–73, 74–75, 78–79
  history of printed, 67
  jackets for, 71, 79
  paper transparency and, 68–69
  pocket, 70, 72–74
  reference, 76
  in a series, 72, 74–76
  show-through and, 68–69
  size of, designer's choice of, 72
  smaller scale grids for, 26, 70
  strike-through and, 68
  textbooks, 74
  typography, 71, 72–73, 74–75
British Library Collection, 68
brochures, 22–23, 26
Burns, Aaron, 78–80, 84

CAD (computer-aided design), 85
Capital, 59–60
catalogues, 22–23, 26
cold-type composition, defined, 85,
  87
Collins, Jeanette, 28, 32
column rules, 39, 63
  elimination of, 30, 37
column width:
  in magazines, 48, 54, 55, 56, 58,
   59–60
  in newspapers, 30, 33
composition, defined, 85
computerized composition, defined,
  85
computers and grids, 26, 81–84
  for book composition, 78–80, 84
  for magazines, 51–53, 62, 82, 84
  for newspapers, 38, 39, 40, 81–84
  for service content, 51–53
  terminology, 85–87
corporate identity program, 22–23,
  26
CRT (cathode ray tube) screens, 81,
  82, 83
cubism, 49

da Vinci, Leonardo, 9, 12, 67
Day, Ed, 76
De Architectura (Vitruvius), 15
De Divina Proportione (Pacioli), 9,
  10, 67
Design, 53, 60
design, history of graphic, 9–17
Design Processing International,
  78–80, 84
de Stijl, 49
de Vries, Jan, 9
direct-entry typesetter, defined, 85
directories, 26
disk, defined, 85
Domus, 53, 60–61
dynamic symmetry, 13–15

Editing and Design—Book 5 (Evans), 30
Elements of Dynamic Symmetry (Hambridge) 13–15
encyclopedias, 76–77
Euclid, 67
Eusebius, 67
Evans, Harold, 30, 33

Fibonacci series, 10, 14
filmsetting, defined, 86
Financial Times, 44
Fleckhaus, Willy, 55, 56
Fletcher, Alan, 44, 46

Germany, 17, 27
Gerstner, Karl, 59–60
Ghyka, Matila, 15
GIGO, defined, 85–86
Glaser, Milton, 62
"golden section," 9–15, 67, 71
Gothic (Old English) style lettering, 28, 29
graphic design, history of, 9–17
grids, 17–26
    for architectural perspective, 9
    for books, 72–73, 74–75, 78–79
    computers and, 26, 38, 39, 40, 51–53, 62
    defined, 9, 86
    development of the modern, 17
    final layout and actual-size, 26, 64
    form and function, 21–26
    history of use of, 9
    Le Corbusier's *Modulor*, 14–17, 26
    nine-unit, 44–45, 46
    orthodox design grid, 21–26
    preliminary sketches using smaller scale, 26
    priorities in designing, 19–21
    six-unit, 36, 40, 48, 55
    the square and, 12–13
    strike-through and show-through in books and, 68–69
    three-unit, 52–53, 61
    twelve-unit, 55, 56, 57, 62

typographic, for books, 72–73, 74–75
Griffo, Francesco, 67, 68
Grimbly, Brian, 60
Gutenberg, Johann, 67, 68, 80

Hambidge, Jay, 13–15
Harris 2200 Visual Display Terminal, 81
headlines, newspaper typography, 31–32, 33, 40, 45
Helvetica type, 40
Homage to the Book (Zapf), 78
Homelife, 51
Hopkins, Will, 57, 59, 62
Hurlburt, Allen, 79
hyphenation, defined, 86

Ictinus, 10
Industrial Design, 52–53, 61
International Typeface Corporation, 78

Japanese tatami mats, 12
Jenson, Nicolaus, 67

L'Architecture d'Aujourd'hui, 16–17
"La Section d'Or," 11
Layout: The Design of the Printed Page (Hurlburt), 79
layout machine, 82
Le Corbusier, 14, 15, 16, 26
letterpress printing, 68
L'Express, 62
Life magazine, 82
line feed, defined, 86
line printer, defined, 86
logotype, 28, 29
London Sunday Times, 30, 32–33
London Times, 28, 32
Look magazine, 53–55, 57, 59

magazines, 48–64
    column makeup, 48, 54, 55, 56, 58, 59–60

computers and composition of, 51–53, 62, 82, 84
content, 49
filmsetting, 50, 51
grid's role in, 51–56, 63–64
headlines, 50
history of layout of, 49–50
horizontal divisions in, 55, 58, 59
metal typesetting, 50
production process, 50–51
six-unit grid, 48, 55
four-unit grid superimposed, 59–60
smaller scale grids for, 26, 64
three-unit grid, 52–53
twelve-unit grid, 56, 57, 62
typographic rules for, 49–50
Manutius, Aldus, 67, 68
mathematics:
design and, 9
"golden section" and, 10
logarithmic spiral, 14, 15
the *Modulor* and, 16–17
the square and, 11, 13
menu, defined, 86
Mergenthaler Linotype Company, 83
Minneapolis Tribune, 40–45
Mitchell Beasley, 76
Modulor, the, 14–17, 26
Mondrian, Piet, 13
Morison, Stanley, 28, 29, 32, 33
Müller-Brockmann, Josef, 21, 26
Munich Olympic games, signage system for, 24–25

Newsday, 35–36
newspapers, 29–46
center fold of, headline and photography layout and, 28
column rules, 30, 37, 39
column width, 30, 33
computer composition of, 38, 39, 40, 81–84
front page summaries of contents, 28
headline typography, 31–32, 33, 40, 45
horizontal influence in design, 30, 32, 37, 39
logotype, 28, 29
modulor form, 28, 31, 33
one-half scale grids for, 26, 42
paragraphing in, 41, 45
placement of important page-one story, 45
tabloid, 35–36
typesize, 30–31, 40, 42
New York Daily News, 83
New York *Herald*, 36–39
New York Herald Tribune, 29, 31, 32
New York magazine, 62
New York Times, 32, 33, 34, 78, 84

OCR (optical character recognition), 81, 86
on-line and off-line, defined, 86
Oppositions, 54

Pacioli, Fra Luca, 9, 10, 67
Palazzo, Peter, 29, 31, 32
paper:
coated and halftone surfaces, 69
lightweight, 68–69
Penguin Books, 70, 74
pentagon, 10
perspective, architectural, 9
Phidias, 10
photocomposition, defined, 86
Pierpont Morgan Library, 67
Plato, 15
pocket books, 70, 72–74
Poe, Edgar Allan, 74–75
Poliphilus, 67, 68
Ponti, Lisa, 60
printout, defined, 86
proportion, 9, 53
in books, 67–68, 69, 71
dynamic symmetry, 13–15
golden section, 9–15
the *Modulor*, 14–17
rules of, 9–17
the square, 10–13

Rand, Paul, 18–19
Random House Encyclopedia, 77
Ratdolt, Erhard, 67
rectangle, 17
    golden, 9–15, 67, 71
    root-2, 11, 13
reference books, 76
Rolling Stone, 63

San Francisco Examiner, 43, 45–46
sans-serif typeface, 46
show-through and grid patterns,
    68–69
signage system, 24–25, 26
Silverstein, Louis, 33, 34, 78, 84
square, the, 10–13
strike-through and grid patterns, 68
Suite de la Modulor, 16–17
Switzerland, 17, 22, 26, 41
System Five Page View Terminal,
    83

tabloids, 35–36
tape, defined, 86
tape merger, defined, 87
tatami mat in Japanese architecture,
    12
Taylor, Edwin, 33
textbooks, 74
Thompson, Bradbury, 72–73, 74
Time magazine, 62–63
Times Roman, 28, 29, 32
Tory, Geofroy, 67
Tschichold, Jan, 67, 70, 71, 74, 81
Twen magazine, 55, 56, 57, 58, 59, 63
24 Ore, 44–45, 46
typesetting methods, 85–87
type size in newspapers, 30–31, 40,
    42
typewriter composition, defined, 87

van de Graaf, 71
VDT (video display terminal), 81–82,
    87

Vignelli, Massimo, 20, 22–23,
    36–39, 52–53, 54, 61
Vitruvius, 15

Wall Street Journal, 44
Wharton, 57
word processing, defined, 87

Zapf, Hermann, 78–80, 84